From Ginger Shaw
on the 3rd year
anniversary of Bill's
death.

3/9/02

1-

DIAMONDS IN THE DARK

DIAMONDS IN THE DARK

JACK GRAHAM

THOMAS NELSON PUBLISHERS
Nashville • Atlanta • London • Vancouver

Copyright © 1997 by Jack Graham

Published in Nashville, Tennessee, by Thomas Nelson, Inc., Publishers, and distributed in Canada by Word Communications, Ltd., Richmond, British Columbia, and in the United Kingdom by Word (UK), Ltd., Milton Keynes, England.

Unless otherwise noted, Scripture quotations are from THE NEW KING JAMES VERSION of the Bible, © 1979, 1980, 1982, Thomas Nelson, Inc., Publishers.

Scripture quotations noted KJV are from the KING JAMES VERSION of the Holy Bible.

Library of Congress Cataloging-in-Publication Data
Graham, Jack, 1950–
    Diamonds in the dark / Jack Graham.
        p. cm.
    ISBN 0-7852-7427-8
    1. Encouragement—Religious aspects—Christianity.   2. Encouragement—Biblical teaching.   3. Bible—Biography.   I. Title.
BV4647.E53G73   1997
242′.4—dc21   96-44464
                                                                              CIP

Printed in the United States of America

2 3 4 5 6 7 BVG 00 99 98 97

To my parents,
Tom and Emogene Graham,
Who never missed a ball game,
never failed to encourage me,
and introduced me to faith.

Against all odds, they raised two sons,
both of us preachers of the gospel.

They taught me to believe
and always look to the light
in spite of the night.

I look forward to joining them one day
in the presence of the Savior,
and in that place where
there is no night.

Table of Contents

◆ ◆ ◆

Foreword

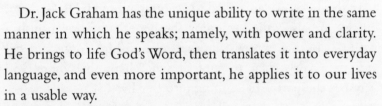

Dr. Jack Graham has the unique ability to write in the same manner in which he speaks; namely, with power and clarity. He brings to life God's Word, then translates it into everyday language, and even more important, he applies it to our lives in a usable way.

As you read *Diamonds in the Dark*, you will find yourself saying, "I relate to that," or "I've been there," or "I know exactly how Elijah or some of the other prophets must have felt. They came out all right and this gives me hope that I too will come out all right." After all, we do worship the same Lord.

Dr. Graham gives us many spiritual insights that enable us to know beyond doubt that the God of heaven is also the One who walked the earth; that the One who hung the stars relates to a broken heart, a troubled mind, and a disturbed lifestyle. As you read you will find yourself feeling the feelings of the various biblical characters and applying them in your own life and in the lives of your friends.

This book is inspiring and encouraging because it is filled with hope and specific suggestions that will lead you straight to the Cross for a heart transplant. *Diamonds in the Dark* is a book that each member of the family will be blessed by reading and, when read as a family, will bring that family closer together.

Using modern language to define old-fashioned sin, Dr. Graham gives us a clear picture of the consequences, whether the sin was committed three thousand years ago or yesterday. Through it all, though, we see God's hand in our lives and have the ongoing assurance that if we belong to Him, everything that happens to us has already crossed His desk and that all things do work together for good to those who love Him.

In this book we are called to accountability by Dr. Graham, but we are also called to enjoy the benefits of a relationship with Christ that exceeds all other relationships. In vivid detail we get a very clear picture of what happens when God "crashes the party" by coming into our lives.

Here's a book that will appeal to your historical sense of lifestyle and give you a sense of awe about the omnipotence of a holy God. It challenges you intellectually, involves you emotionally, and ultimately, through biblical stories, examples, and promises, leads you closer to Christ as Lord, Savior, and Master.

Dr. Graham skillfully brings the men of thousands of years ago, and the lessons they taught through the lives they lived, into the present time and makes their faith as real today as it was then. In the process, our eyes are opened to the promises of God, the love of God, and the privilege we have of glorifying and serving Him.

Zig Ziglar
Dallas, Texas

Introduction

Through the years, some of my most remarkable encounters with God have been at night.

Being a "night person," I am often alert to spiritual light in those quiet evening hours. I recall, as a youth, meeting God at evening camp services or during great revival meetings in my home church.

It was on a Sunday night that I walked forward at the invitation of my pastor and responded to God's call to preach the gospel. In those days, there were even times of lying out under the stars on hot summer evenings in Texas and contemplating the greatness and glory of the Creator. He seemed so near. As I looked at the stars penetrating the night sky, they looked like diamonds in the darkness.

There have also been dark times emotionally in which God's grace burst through the night, exposing me to His incomparable presence. The Lord Jesus has been very real to me during some dark days and long nights. Each time, I have seen diamonds in the darkness.

In the Word of God, we cannot help noticing the times when men and women had fresh encounters with the living Lord in the darkest times. Out of my own experience, I observed in the Scriptures that when God's saints were plunged into the night, He appeared with night light.

The Christian life is not all sunshine. In fact, the greatest lessons of life are often learned when life's shadows fall. God teaches us in the light, but He tests us in the night. Christian character is developed in the dark. So if you are in a night season right now, congratulations! You are about to experience this glorious light.

I have written this book with the prayer that each reader will be encouraged by the Lord, who is our light and our salvation. May all who read these words discover the reality of His supernatural presence and share, with me, diamonds in the darkness!

CHAPTER 1

Broken in the Night, Blessed in the Light:
JACOB'S WRESTLING MATCH

Have you ever been afraid at night? Have you ever felt lost, lonely, or confused in the dark? Maybe you have lain awake in bed at night during a bad storm, wishing the lightning and thunder would stop and the morning would hurry up and come.

When I was a child, I was afraid of the dark. Even Davy Crockett and Howdy Doody, my boyhood heroes from the fifties, could not help me when things went bump in the night. I had a Howdy Doody doll I would hug at night. I had a Davy Crockett coonskin cap and gun and the whole outfit. But I was still afraid of the dark.

Most of us simply don't enjoy darkness all that much. In the dark, there are all kinds of noises. We exaggerate things all out of proportion. So often at nighttime we relive the frustrations, problems, and cares that cause us to struggle emotionally and spiritually.

Maybe you have recently experienced a "dark night of the soul." You may even be in a dark time in your life right now, wondering what happened and trying to find your way back to the light.

If any of these emotions or experiences are familiar to you, I have two important things to share with you. First, you are perfectly normal. Every one of us has had occasion to fear the dark. God's people are not exempt from the dark times, as we are going to see often in this book. If you have ever been fearful or frustrated or lonely or lost in the dark, welcome to the family.

The second thing I want to share with you is much more important than the first. If you are a child of God, you need to know that He will meet you in your night place.

In fact, there is a unique Scripture that tells us there are times when the God who dwells in glorious light can be found in the darkness: "Moses drew near the thick darkness where God was" (Ex. 20:21). You might say God works the night shift. Solomon said, "The LORD said He would dwell in the dark cloud" (2 Chron. 6:1).

God often leads us into the darkness—not to frighten or abandon us, but so that we might see the glory and the power of His presence in a way we could never see it in the light. Isaiah 50:10 advises us, "Who among you fears the LORD? Who obeys the voice of His Servant? Who walks in darkness and has no light? Let him trust in the name of the LORD and rely upon his God." The fact is that God's love often shines more brightly and more beautifully in the dark than at any other time in our lives.

In the chapters ahead we will see this truth unfolded in the lives of men like Elijah, Jonah, Daniel, Peter, and Paul. But I want to begin with one of the most intriguing and colorful people in all of Scripture, the patriarch Jacob.

This man had a nighttime encounter with God in which he seemed to lose everything, only to discover that he had gained it all. But Jacob's discovery did not come without a price. We are going to meet a man who was broken in the night, that he might be blessed in the light.

The "Heel-Catcher"

Before we follow Jacob into the darkness, we need to know a little bit about him. He was the second of twin sons born to Isaac and Rebekah (Gen. 25:19–26). Rebekah was barren, so Isaac "pleaded with the LORD for his wife" (v. 21). God answered Isaac's prayer and gave this couple two beautiful baby boys, Esau and Jacob.

But something was wrong even in the womb, because Rebekah felt the boys struggling inside of her. Esau and Jacob were fighting even before they were born. Rebekah asked the Lord what was happening, and He explained that there were two nations in her womb. The older brother would serve the younger, a scenario that always spells big trouble (Gen. 25:22–23).

At birth, Esau came out first, with Jacob literally gripping his heel. Esau was red-haired, so he was given a name that means "the hairy one" or "the red one." Jacob was named "the heel-catcher, the supplanter"—in other words, the one who trips you up, the ambusher.

No name was ever more appropriate, for Jacob was in fact a deceitful man, a cheat, and a conniver all the days of his youth. Many years later the prophet Jeremiah, when seeking to describe the treachery of the human heart, would use the root word from which Jacob's name is derived to say, "The heart is deceitful [literally, "The heart is a Jacob"] above all things . . ." (Jer. 17:9).

That is pretty amazing when you think about it. It's the equivalent of saying if you looked up the word *deceit* in the dictionary, you would find Jacob's picture. Jacob had the heart of a cheater, and he lived up to his name by cheating and conning his way through life.

For example, Jacob conned Esau out of his family birthright by waving food under his older brother's nose when he was hungry (Gen. 25:29–34). And he connived and conspired with Rebekah to trick the blind and aged Isaac into giving him the blessing instead of Esau (Gen. 27:1–40).

As a result of all these deceptive acts, Esau vowed to kill his brother (Gen. 27:41). So Jacob did what most deceivers and con men do when they're found out. He ran away. He skipped town. That's important, because when Jacob ran away from Esau he was using the one ploy that he thought could always get him out of trouble.

My purpose here is not to recount the entire story of Jacob. In Genesis 28–31, you can read the account of his flight to the house of Laban and all the events that happened to him there. It's interesting that when Rebekah told Jacob to get away until Esau's anger had cooled, she said, "This will all blow over in a few days, son" (see Gen. 27:43–44).

Not exactly. Jacob was gone for twenty years. During that time he tangled again and again with Laban, a man who was a pretty good deceiver in his own right. Jacob wound up marrying Laban's daughters Leah and Rachel, which meant that God gave the great conniver a conniver for a father-in-law!

When things got too hot for Jacob in Laban's house, Jacob did what he did best: He took his family and ran. Only this time he decided to run back to his homeland and face his family, and this is where I want to pick up the story. Jacob sent messengers ahead of him to find out if Esau was still angry with him after those twenty long years (Gen. 32:3–5).

No More Tricks, No Place to Run

The messengers brought back bad news (Gen. 32: 6). Esau had gathered four hundred men and was coming out to meet Jacob. To Jacob, this could only mean one thing. Esau was still angry with him, and was coming out to kill him.

Finally, after all the lies and deceit, Jacob was at the end of his rope. He had no more tricks up the sleeve of his robe, and no place to run. This is where I want to pick up the narrative in Genesis 32, beginning with verse 22: "And [Jacob] arose that night and took his two wives, his two female servants, and his eleven sons, and crossed over the ford of Jabbok. He took them, sent them over the brook, and sent over what he had. Then Jacob was left alone."

Alone in the Darkness

Jacob was finally alone in the darkness. Everyone he loved and everything he possessed was on the other side of the brook at Jabbok. He had come to the end of his scheming. All of the sins of the past had caught up with him. He was alone in the darkness; praying, worrying, trying to figure things out, perhaps reflecting on his past, remembering all the things he had done, not knowing what to do there in the darkness.

But this is just where God wanted Jacob to be, because the trickster was about to become a wrestler: Jacob was about to enter into an all-night wrestling match with God, a fierce fight for supremacy in Jacob's life. This was to be the defining moment for Jacob, for he was now at the breaking point.

A Desperate Struggle

As Jacob lay there under the stars, dreading facing Esau the next morning and praying that God would somehow spare his life, someone attacked him. Suddenly, without warning, the Bible says Jacob found himself locked in a desperate struggle with "a Man" (Gen. 32:24).

At the outset of the fight, Jacob didn't have a clue who his opponent was. He must have wondered, "Who in the world has got hold of me?" Maybe he thought it was Esau, coming out of the shadows to finish Jacob off himself. Maybe it was one of Esau's men sent to ambush him.

Some people in those days believed that demons lived around creeks, so perhaps Jacob thought one of those demons had jumped on him. The rabbis of Israel used to say that the angel who attacked Jacob on that evening was his guardian angel. Now that's humorous to me. Imagine a man so despicable in character that his own guardian angel attacks him!

It wasn't long, however, until Jacob realized he was not fighting a man or even an angel. This had to be none other than *the* angel, the "Angel of the Lord." Most Bible scholars believe this was a preincarnate appearance of the Lord Jesus Himself, and so do I. Jacob was wrestling with God, for later he would say, "I have seen God face to face" (Gen. 32: 30).

Imagine how surprised Jacob must have been when he realized whom he was fighting. Of all the people Jacob might have expected to come out of the shadows and grab him that night, I suspect that God was at the bottom of the list.

But God has a way of showing up at the most unexpected times in the most unexpected places. This kind of thing had happened once before in Jacob's life. Back in Genesis 28:10–11, when Jacob was fleeing from Esau, he put a stone under his head for a pillow and went to sleep.

Then Jacob had a dream in which he saw a ladder reaching into heaven, with the angels of God ascending and descending on it. When he awoke, Jacob said, "Surely the LORD is in this place, and I did not know it" (Gen. 28:16). So often God meets us at unexpected times in unexpected places, and here at Peniel, Jacob once again met God suddenly and unexpectedly.

Battling the Lord

Let's think about this scene for a minute. Jacob was praying for God to help him, and God attacked him. Has that ever happened to you? You pray, "Oh God, help me! Deliver me! Get me out of this one!" But God sends you more trouble, more problems, added pain, further heartache. Why would He do that?

It could be that God wants you to learn the lesson He was teaching Jacob. You see, Jacob's problem wasn't Esau. His problem was God. Jacob had been resisting God all of his life. He had been living his life independently of God, and now God was bringing him to the end of himself.

Jacob's rebellious heart needed to be broken so he could be blessed. I think Jacob realized this was a make-or-break situation for him, because even though the Lord dislocated Jacob's hip and said, "Let Me go," Jacob held on and cried out, "I will not let You go unless You bless me!" (Gen. 32:25–26).

Sometimes, as Christians, it seems that our toughest battles are with God and not with the devil. Can you identify with that? I think all of us can say that at certain times in our lives, we find ourselves locked in a painful wrestling match with God. Why is that? What is the problem?

I believe it is because God wants to bring every one of us into complete dependence upon Himself, yet we want to depend upon ourselves. From childhood, just like Jacob the "heel-catcher," we say, "I can do it myself." If we don't mature spiritually, we end up living independently of God, trying to scheme and connive our way through life.

Go into any bookstore today and look in the self-help section. You'll find all kinds of books telling you how to better yourself, promote yourself, be good to yourself, reward yourself, be your own best friend, and on and on. This generation has grown up with a self-help mentality, so today we have self-service gas, self-service food, even self-service banking with our ATM cards.

There is an independent streak in every one of us. There is a Jacob in every heart, a part of us that says, "I'm going to do it my way." But God will not allow us, as His children, to do it our way. If we will not submit our way and will to God's, He will bring us to the end of ourselves that He might strip us of our selfishness and self-centeredness.

Why? Because God wants to get the "Jacob" out of us. He wants to take the phoniness and the hypocrisy and the conniving out of our character so He can conform us to the image of the Lord Jesus Christ. This is a battle we all face, one that I pray we don't win.

As we will see in the life of Jacob, it's only as we surrender to the Lord and concede the battle that we actually win.

It is only in losing ourselves that we find ourselves. Jacob was locked in the battle of his life. He couldn't con his way out of it. He couldn't run from it, so he hung on for dear life.

Time for Surrender

As the day started to break (in other words, as Jacob's time in the darkness was about to end), "[The Angel] said to him, 'What is your name?' He said, 'Jacob'" (Gen. 32:27).

Now that was a very important question. The Lord knew Jacob's name, but He wanted Jacob to admit who he was. In the very saying of his name, Jacob would be admitting that he was the consummate schemer.

Someone said that adversity introduces you to yourself. So often in the darkness, in the struggles of life, we come face-to-face with who God is and who we are, including our past, our sin, and our deceit.

So Jacob and God wrestled all night. Have you wondered why God allowed Jacob to prevail against Him? God could have crushed him at any time. But God allowed Jacob to hang on because He was waiting for Jacob to surrender. God was waiting for Jacob to deal with his stubbornness and self-ishness. You see, Jacob was not grappling with God, but with himself. He was wrestling with his own spirit.

As the morning light began to break, the Angel put a "heavenly hold" on Jacob and Jacob's thigh bone was pulled out of its socket. The thigh bone is the largest bone in the body, the running bone. Now Jacob couldn't run anymore. God had finally chased him down, and now God had brought him down. Now Jacob was broken.

But it was in his pain and in his suffering that Jacob cried out, "I will not let You go unless You bless me!" This was what God wanted to hear all along. This was Jacob's confession, his surrender. He was at the point of desperation where he realized that unless the Lord did something, he wouldn't make it.

Receiving the Blessing

So God answered Jacob's prayer and blessed him. In the Old Testament, the blessing was the transfer of power. From now on, the power of God would rest upon this man. God also gave Jacob two things to remind him of this experience: a new name, "Israel," meaning "prince with God," and a painful limp. He would carry both of them the rest of his life.

Brokenness and Blessing

Do you see the point here? Israel got the blessing and the power of God at the same time he acquired his limp. God had to break him in the darkness to bless him in the light. Look at Genesis 32:31. The sun was just beginning to shine on Israel as he crossed the brook, limping on his dislocated hip. He was broken, but he was also blessed.

Can you imagine what Jacob must have looked like that morning as he rejoined his family? His hair is messed up, he has dirt all over him, his clothes are torn, and he is limping! Someone asks him, "What in the world has happened to you?"

Jacob smiles and says, "I just got blessed."

Paul had a similar experience that he called his "thorn in the flesh," his version of Jacob's limp (2 Cor. 12:7). Paul asked God three times to take the thorn away, to stop the pain. I don't think these were bland little prayers. I believe Paul wrestled with God in agonizing prayer about this thing.

But God used that thorn as a strange minister. What seemed to be a monster became a minister to Paul, for God told him, "My grace is sufficient for you" (2 Cor. 12:9). Through it all Paul learned the lesson we all need to learn in the darkness: "When I am weak, then I am strong" (2 Cor. 12:10).

So here was Jacob, tattered and torn and limping—but a new man! It's significant that when Jacob's portrait is hung in God's "Hall of Faith" in Hebrews 11, of all the things that could have been said about him as one of the heroes of the faith, the writer of Hebrews recorded this: "By faith Jacob . . . worshiped, leaning on the top of his staff" (v. 21).

Strength in Weakness

Jacob walked with a limp; he had to lean on a crutch when he stood up. He walked with a reminder of the time when he came face-to-face with God, and God broke him in order that He might bless him.

Jacob learned what we need to learn, that every pain is a reminder of our dependence on the Lord. Every time Jacob's hip ached, the ache whispered, "You are no longer the same man. You have been changed. You have been made new." Jacob couldn't run anymore. He couldn't connive and cheat the way he used to connive and cheat. All he could do was walk in obedience to and in fellowship with God.

Broken in the Right Place

Jacob's pain was divine discomfort. He was broken, but he was broken in the right place. Now it is possible to be broken in the wrong place. You can be broken and become bitter, harsh, and defeated. You can be broken and become faithless. You can be broken and abandon all hope.

When God breaks you, He will always break you in the right place. His purpose is not to embitter you, but to bless you; not to weaken you, but to make you stronger at the broken place.

When I was six years of age, I was out skating one day when I hit a crack in the sidewalk and went flying. I landed hard on the sidewalk and when I got up, something was wrong with my arm. It was all crooked, and I couldn't feel it.

I was pretty sure what had happened, so I went in to my mom, held up my arm, and said, "Mom, I think I broke my arm." She screamed like any good mother would, and we ran to the doctor. I remember thinking, "I am not going to cry. I am going to tell all my friends that I broke my arm, but I didn't cry." And I didn't cry. It hurt, but I never cried.

The doctor set my arm and put it in a cast for about six weeks. At first, it was kind of neat to have that cast. It was a good weapon, and all the girls wanted to sign it. But after about four weeks, that thing started itching. I was sticking coat hangers in there trying to scratch it. And I couldn't swing a bat or throw a ball, so I was ready to get rid of that cast.

When I got my cast off, I was so happy. I felt like a bird let out of its cage. I went home, got out my little red wagon, put one knee in that wagon and the other foot on the ground, and took off flying down the sidewalk.

You'll never guess what happened. I flipped over and broke my arm again. Then the very day I got that second cast off, I broke the same arm a third time. This time I cried.

My arm was broken a second and third time in the same place because it was still weak from the previous break. But as those bones healed, they got stronger. I am told that when broken bones heal, they actually get stronger at the broken place.

That is what God does with us. He breaks us at the right place in our lives, at the point of our sin and stubbornness and rebellion. It is painful to be broken, but if we will allow God to break us, He will then make us stronger at the broken place. That's what He did to Jacob.

So the question is, Do you want the blessing of God upon your life? Be careful how you answer, because if you want God's blessing you must pay the price in surrender and brokenness before Him.

A Test of Brokenness

What does it mean to be broken before the Lord? Here is a checklist of questions you can ask yourself as you search your heart and seek God's blessing:

- ♦ Am I willing to let go of my dreams and ambitions if such is the will of God for me?
- ♦ Am I defensive when accused or criticized, or even when I am misunderstood?
- ♦ Am I coveting what others have instead of waiting on God's provision for my life?
- ♦ Am I forgiving when I am offended, even when I don't receive an apology?
- ♦ Am I always talking about my rights; that is, rights I have not surrendered to the Lord and given up?
- ♦ Am I thinking of others first, out of love?
- ♦ Am I proudly appearing that I am always right and always have the answer?

- ♦ Am I practicing the daily spiritual disciplines of prayer, Bible study, worship, and solitude?
- ♦ Am I being silent regarding self-promotion, allowing God to do my public relations instead of promoting myself?
- ♦ Am I praying each day, "God, whatever it takes, I am willing to submit to Your leadership"?
- ♦ Am I expressing joy in the difficulties and circumstances of life that God uses to change and refine me?
- ♦ Am I taking risks in obedience to Christ instead of giving in to fear and denial and pride?

These are penetrating questions, but questions we must constantly ask ourselves. It is only when we come to a point of surrender and brokenness before the Lord, when our lives are laid bare before Him, that God can begin to change us and heal us and make the broken places strong.

Then with every step we take, our limp will remind us of our weakness and humility before God. Someone has eloquently described the "Jacob" experience we must all undergo if we are to be used mightily by God:

> When God wants to drill a man
> And thrill a man
> And skill a man, when God wants to mold a man
> To play the noblest part; when he yearns with all his heart
> To create so bold and great a man, that all the world shall
>   be amazed, watch His methods, watch His ways.
> How He ruthlessly perfects
> Whom He royally elects.
> How He hammers him and hurts him, and
> With mighty blows converts him

Into trial shapes of clay which
Only God understands. While his tortured heart is crying,
  and he lifts beseeching hands.
How He bends but never breaks, when his good He
  undertakes; How he uses whom he chooses
And with every purpose fuses him; By every act induces him
  to try his splendor out—God knows what He's about.

(J. Oswald Sanders, *Spiritual Leadership*,
© 1967, Mood, p. 141)

Are you in a dark time in your life? Are you facing struggles that seem to have leaped upon you out of the darkness? Are you wrestling with God? Hold on to Him until you are ready to give in to His will and receive His blessing. When you do, God will take your brokenness and bless you beyond measure.

CHAPTER 2

Coming out of the Cave:
ELIJAH'S NEAR "CAVE-IN"

Genuine heroes seem to be in short supply in America these days. But one emerged from the woods of Bosnia in the summer of 1995, and the nation erupted in cheers.

He was a young Air Force captain named Scott O'Grady, whose fighter plane was shot down by Serbian rebels. O'Grady parachuted from the crippled aircraft and eluded his would-be captors for six days, eating insects and drinking rainwater to survive before being rescued by a Marine helicopter.

Scott O'Grady was not looking to be a hero. He did not ask for the life-threatening situation he found himself in. But O'Grady, a committed Christian, emerged from it with his life intact. And he said he learned to trust God in a dynamic new way. In a dark place where God was all he had, O'Grady found out that God was all he needed.

The prophet Elijah learned that same lesson in his dark place. He didn't choose the life-threatening darkness that engulfed him. He was being hunted not by enemy soldiers, but by the rulers of Israel. In 1 Kings 19:9, we find the great prophet in a cave at Mount Horeb, the ancient name for Mount Sinai.

How Elijah got there, and what God did to bring him out with his life and ministry intact, is a fascinating story. It's also a lesson from Scripture filled with principles we can use during those times in our lives when the darkness seems to swallow us.

The Despondent Prophet

Elijah was despondent, discouraged, and even depressed. Now when I say Elijah was depressed, I'm not talking about clinical depression, an illness that requires professional medical treatment. I'm referring to those periods we all have when we are physically or emotionally drained and the darkness overtakes us. Times like these are a normal part of life.

While they are sure to come, such times are still painful. All of us can identify with Elijah's feelings from time to time, so let's learn from his example.

A Great Victory

Believe it or not, the root of Elijah's depression lay in a great victory that secured his reputation as a fearless prophet. Israel was ruled by the spineless King Ahab and his wicked wife, Queen Jezebel. They had introduced Baal worship into Israel, sustaining hundreds of prophets of Baal at their own table.

God sent Elijah to challenge Israel's paganism, and in a great contest on Mount Carmel, Elijah stood alone against 450 Baal prophets in the sight of all Israel (1 Kings 18:19–20). There he built an altar to the Lord, and in answer to Elijah's prayer, the fire of God fell and consumed the sacrifice (1 Kings 18:38). The people fell on their faces and confessed, "The LORD, He is God!" (1 Kings 18:39). All of the evil prophets were then executed.

So the enemies of the people of God were destroyed and defeated as Israel underwent a tremendous spiritual awakening and revival. Elijah's victory on Mount Carmel stands as one of the greatest spiritual victories in all of Scripture. God singularly used this man Elijah as His instrument on that day.

A Serious Threat

When Queen Jezebel heard of what happened at Carmel, she threatened the life of this great prophet of God. And rather than standing strong and confident and courageous as he had done just a few days earlier, Elijah ran for his life (1 Kings 19:1–3). He knew Jezebel meant every word of her threat.

Elijah became fearful, anxious, and afraid, and he ran over thirty miles into the desert. That's where we find him in 1 Kings 19: "But [Elijah] himself went a day's journey into the wilderness, and came and sat down under a broom tree" (v. 4).

I'm glad the Scripture tells us the truth about the great saints of God. Just like you and me, Elijah and others who have faithfully served the Lord God faced times of deep physical, emotional, and spiritual need. It is possible to be serving the Lord and yet find yourself emotionally and mentally drained, depleted, and depressed.

Often, we put the great men and women of Scripture on a pedestal, but the Bible clearly tells us that Elijah "was a man with a nature like ours" (James 5:17). That means he was susceptible to physical and emotional breakdown just like any other child of God. Elijah knew what it was like to feel the darkness descend and wrap itself around him.

A Hasty Retreat

Faced with Jezebel's threat, Elijah chose to turn his face away and run for his life into the desert. By the time he stopped running and fell exhausted under a broom, or juniper tree, he had sunk into a dark hole of depression. He even prayed, "It is enough! Now, LORD, take my life, for I am no better than my fathers!" (1 Kings 19:4b). And he's not even at the cave yet!

The Symptoms of Depression

You may read these opening verses of 1 Kings 19 and say, "Yes, that's me, all right. I know exactly how Elijah felt. I've been there. I can identify with his feelings." Now as I said earlier, I think all of us have experienced these same kinds of feelings from time to time. They are part of the human condition.

The problem comes when these feelings of depression come and don't leave, when they begin to dominate our lives. If you are in that situation right now, if the darkness refuses to lift, it may be time to seek professional help.

The darkness that is clinical depression may have a physical cause, for which there is medical help. There is also help available for the emotional and spiritual components of serious depression. Let me urge you again to seek help if you are battling a depression that rest and refreshment cannot alleviate.

We are going to see that Elijah's condition had all three components—physical, emotional, and spiritual—and that God dealt with each one in turn. Through this we are going to discover real help and hope from the Scriptures for lifting the darkness that engulfs us all from time to time.

Physical Exhaustion

Elijah certainly manifested many of the classic symptoms of a person with normal depression. He was fatigued and listless. He had not only lost his zest for life and sense of purpose he had exhibited just a few days earlier on Mount Carmel, he had even lost his will to live.

Elijah was no longer interested in being the man of God, standing firm against evil. He no longer seemed to care that Israel was still in the clutches of Ahab and Jezebel. A sense of hopelessness and helplessness had enveloped him. Fear and anxiety were clutching at his spirit. His thoughts had turned to death as his best way of escape.

These kinds of feelings are usually a reaction to some loss, tragedy, or problem in a person's life: the loss of health, the loss of a loved one, the loss of a job, the death of a dream, deep grief that will not go away, or some other setback. When the problem hits and the pressure mounts, then depression can set in.

Let's look at Elijah's problem, because in it we may find help in understanding our problems and where to look for help when the darkness won't go away. We have already suggested one of Elijah's problems. He was physically exhausted.

Elijah had just experienced a very demanding and taxing few days. The contest on Carmel was a great triumph, but I don't mean to suggest that it was a cakewalk. We can only imagine the amount of physical stamina it took for Elijah to withstand the overwhelming odds against him.

So Elijah had expended a tremendous amount of energy. He had been zealous for the Lord. Then he ran more than the equivalent of a Boston Marathon into the desert to escape Jezebel. His strength was gone. He was tired. He was lonely. He was worn out and burned out, at the breaking point.

That sounds like the day we live in. Many of us today are piling hours on top of hours at work and even at home, and the responsibilities of modern life are wearing people out. We are seeing lives in meltdown all around us.

When we are physically exhausted, when we are not sleeping well or eating right or exercising properly, when our nerves are frayed by anxiety and fear, we become candidates for depression. That's exactly what happened to Elijah. He was physically wasted.

Emotional Stress

Elijah's physical stress was compounded by severe emotional stress. We can see this very clearly in 1 Kings 19:4, where he said, "LORD, take my life, for I am no better than my fathers!"

Elijah was frustrated and angry. What he was saying was, "Lord, I've had it. You've brought me to the end. You might as well get it over with and kill me before Jezebel does. I thought I was Your prophet. I thought I was special to You. But I'm no better off than anyone else."

So here's Elijah, tired and irritated and mad. Depression is often linked to irritation and impatience and anger turned inward. And yet people who are depressed often say, "No, I'm not angry about anything."

Psychologists tell us that depression is often the result of suppressed anger. If we're not careful we can internalize our anger and subconsciously become bitter. Throw in a generous dose of self-pity, which Elijah also exhibited, and you've got a can't-miss formula for depression: self-pity + irritation **X** anger = depression.

Now Elijah was clearly a man of passion and great spiritual power. I would call him an extrovert. We usually think of a depressed person as the melancholy type, the morose kind of person, the introverted personality.

But if an extrovert turns that extroverted personality inward, the results can be devastating. Elijah had risen to the top, all the way to the top of Mount Carmel. The fire of God fell at his word, and God used him to turn Israel back to Himself.

Then Elijah hit bottom as fast as he had risen to the top. And when a passionate, powerful, extroverted person hits bottom, he usually hits it with a thud. Whether you're introverted or extroverted, it can happen to you.

Now Elijah prayed to die, but his heart wasn't really in that prayer. How do I know? Because if he really wanted to die, he would have stayed put and let Jezebel take care of that for him. But in his depressed state, Elijah became obsessed with the idea of dying. "Lord, let me off at this stop. I'm ready to check out."

One of the worst things a person in Elijah's condition can do is to withdraw from everyone and just run away and hide. Of course, Elijah did have a "contract" out on his life; that was a motivating factor in his flight.

For most of us, however, when the darkness is the thickest, we need to force ourselves to be with the people who love and care about us. Believe me, when you're deep in a cavern and the lights are out, it's awfully reassuring to hear the voice of your guide and the whispers of others and know that you're not alone down there!

But when we get in a spot like the one Elijah was in, it's easy to start taking our eyes off the Lord and off the call He has given each one of us. Then we start fretting about self, about circumstances, or about what other people are saying and thinking about us.

If you are the kind of person who is obsessive about everything because you want people to approve of you and like you for who you are and what you do, you will be in for a big emotional letdown if you don't get that approval. And it will happen, because no one can please everybody.

Elijah certainly didn't get any applause for who he was and what he did on Mount Carmel—except from God. But the prophet allowed his fears to well up within him until the anxiety finally put him under.

Meeting Physical and Emotional Needs

So here are the physical and emotional components of Elijah's depression. Now as I indicated above, the prophet's condition also had a spiritual component. However, I want to save that portion of the story for the end of this chapter, because it comes last in the sequence of what God did for Elijah in 1 Kings 19. Before Elijah got to the cave, God took care of his physical and emotional needs.

Rest and Refreshment

The first thing God did to deal with Elijah's depression was to refresh him (1 Kings 19:6–8). He sent an angel with a cake and a jar of water—the first "angel food cake" recorded in the Bible! Elijah had a good meal, got some more sleep, then ate again. The food and the sleep replenished the prophet's exhausted supply of strength and energy.

A French philosopher is reputed to have said, "I have so much to do today, I simply must go to bed!" Sometimes, the most spiritual thing you can do is to take a good nap. When you are physically tired and emotionally drained, you are vulnerable to depression. The darkness looks even darker when you're wiped out.

Dealing with the Emotions

When the dark clouds of depression are clinging to us as they were clinging to Elijah, one of the most important things we can do in the healing process is to admit our depression. That's hard to do for us as Christians, because it sounds so unspiritual to say we are depressed.

But as long as we refuse to admit the fact that we're down and discouraged, we will find ourselves coming out on the short end of a very long stick. It's even possible that our refusal to recognize where we are can be a form of resisting God. Why? Because He may want us to admit our need so we will surrender the fight and allow Him to begin the healing process.

This is important because depression is not the end of the world. Elijah thought it was the end of his world, but God had something better for him. Chances are, God is not through with you either. That means even though you may be in the darkness now, you will get through it. The clouds will lift.

In fact, just admitting what's wrong and surrendering the fight can be a key to real healing. But if you deny that you have a problem, your feelings will be intensified. So it's important to recognize when you're down and take appropriate action, even if it is just to get some rest or a little exercise.

Realize, too, that these things can take time. If it took you a long time to get depressed, it's going to take you a while to get out of the depression.

It is a bit like charging a battery. If a battery is low, you can put a short charge on it and it will be all right for a brief while. But the best way to charge a battery is a long, slow charge. That's the best way to recover too. It takes time, so be willing to wait on God.

The Spiritual Side of Depression

Isn't it interesting that after Elijah got some rest and the angel ministered to him, he was able to travel for forty more days and nights, going all the way to Horeb (1 Kings 19:8)? He was obviously refreshed and strengthened after his more immediate needs were met.

But there was still a dark cloud hanging over Elijah, because he also had a spiritual problem that needed to be dealt with. "And there he went into a cave, and spent the night in that place; and behold, the word of the LORD came to him, and He said to him, 'What are you doing here, Elijah?'" (1 Kings 19:9).

Greater Vulnerability

That was a good question. Elijah was not supposed to be in that cave.

Have you ever observed that we're often the most vulnerable to spiritual defeat right after a great spiritual victory? Elijah had just experienced the mountaintop experience of a lifetime, and now he's plunged into the depths of despair. Often after a supercharged spiritual experience, we find ourselves feeling drained and empty.

Even the Lord Jesus Christ, going about from place to place and performing miracles, felt power go out from His body when a woman came up behind Him in a crowd and touched the hem of His garment (Luke 8:46). He turned around and asked who it was that touched Him, because He felt the release of energy.

As a pastor, I can testify that standing up and preaching Sundays, pouring your heart out and doing spiritual battle, can be a physically exhausting and spiritually draining experience. It's hard to describe what happens unless you've experienced it. I call it a strange, power-going-out-of-you kind of experience.

To me, preaching is like the seventh game of the World Series, the NBA finals, and the Super Bowl all rolled into one. It is a serious experience to preach with lives hanging in the balance. As a preacher, you give of yourself physically, emotionally, and spiritually to the point that you realize your only source of strength and spiritual power is the Holy Spirit.

There have been times when I felt so weak and powerless I didn't even feel like stepping into the pulpit. But I've found that it's in those moments of my greatest weakness that the Holy Spirit often ministers through me with the greatest power.

Elijah needed spiritual restoration as well as physical and emotional restoration, because part of his problem was spiritual. He wasn't supposed to be under the broom tree, and he wasn't supposed to be traveling even farther from home by going on down to Horeb. But he did, and he wound up in the cave.

That is where we often find ourselves, isn't it? The devil knows your greatest weakness. That's important to understand, because we are in a spiritual battle. If the enemy knows your weakness, he will exploit it to his advantage.

In my estimation, two of the devil's chief weapons are discouragement and depression. If he can put you out of the battle by wiping you out emotionally and spiritually, if he can nullify your testimony for Christ, he can turn you into a spiritual casualty.

The devil often uses a weakness, a fear, or a vulnerability in our lives to cause us to lapse into despair and failure. Since God has not given us a spirit of fear, if we are fearful and anxious we can be sure these things did not come from God.

Facing the Issue

So even though Elijah had regained his physical stamina, he was still in the darkness because he was out of God's will. Therefore, after God refreshed Elijah, He rebuked him by asking, "What are you doing here, Elijah?" In other words, "Why aren't you back there serving Me? What are you doing hiding out here in the wilderness? Why did you run away?"

Elijah's answer reveals that he was still feeling twinges of depression: "I have been very zealous for the LORD God of hosts; for the children of Israel have forsaken Your covenant, torn down Your altars, and killed Your prophets with the sword. I alone am left; and they seek to take my life" (1 Kings 19:10).

Elijah tried to defend his actions, and indulged in a little self-pity. I find it interesting that God didn't respond to Elijah's complaint. He simply told him, "Go out, and stand on the mountain before the LORD" (1 Kings 19:11).

After a tremendous demonstration of His power (1 Kings 19:11–12), God spoke to Elijah in the famous "still small voice." God was reminding His fearful prophet that He was still firmly in control of the elements. Elijah didn't need a pyrotechnics display to know how great God was. He had seen the Lord answer by fire on Mount Carmel.

A Word from God

Elijah needed to be still and know that God was still on His throne (Ps. 46:10). The prophet was all fearful and fretful and restless. He needed to hear the call of God on his life once again. He heard it in the still small voice.

At first glance, verses 13–14 make you think you've lost your place and are reading the same thing again. They are identical to verses 9–10. Why did God ask Elijah the same question a second time? And why did Elijah give the same answer?

It's as if God was saying, "All right, Elijah, you've just seen a reminder of My power and majesty, and you've heard My voice calling you once again. So now that you know all of this, let Me ask you again: What are you doing here?"

Elijah's answer showed that he still didn't get the picture. He was still in the dark spiritually. So God spoke again, only this time He gave Elijah no more object lessons:

> Go, return on your way to the Wilderness of Damascus; and when you arrive, anoint Hazael as king over Syria. Also you shall anoint Jehu the son of Nimshi as king over Israel. And Elisha the son of Shaphat of Abel Meholah you shall anoint as prophet in your place.

> (1 Kings 19:15–16)

This time there was no argument. God simply said to Elijah, "Go back to your prophetic ministry. I have some important things for you to do. And by the way, you're not alone. I have seven thousand other people who haven't bowed down to Baal or kissed his image" (see 1 Kings 19:18).

This time, Elijah obeyed and went back (1 Kings 19:19). The darkness was lifted. The depression was over. He had come out of the cave into the light of God's restoring grace and power.

If you are in the cave right now, if the darkness is hanging heavy all around you, you need to wait on the Lord for the renewal of your strength (Isa. 40:31). The strength you need can be found in His Word.

A dear friend of mine who has suffered bouts of depression told me that when he's depressed, he opens his Bible and reviews the many verses he has underlined and the passages he has marked as God speaks to him through His Word.

Often when we are in the darkness, we neglect to read the Word of God. We forget to listen to Him. But when you are in the dark cave of depression, when you are down, discouraged, and defeated, the Spirit of God can use His Word to energize, vitalize, and encourage you, and to keep you going when it seems you can't go another step.

So God refreshed, rebuked, and recommissioned Elijah. He still had something important for Elijah to do. When we are depressed, we often feel life is over. There is nothing left to do. But when we listen to God, He comes to say, "I have a purpose in life for you. There is something wonderful for you to do, so get up! Be renewed! Go in My authority and power."

You see, the ultimate cure for the "everyday" kind of depression we wrestle with is the healing hand of God, whether in physical rest and refreshment, emotional healing, or the spiritual therapy of the truth in His Word. Often, it requires all three!

When you're in the cave, it may seem like you'll never come out. Elijah was renewed physically, but he wasn't really "fixed" until he got his spiritual bearings outside that cave at Horeb. Then the last cloud of despair and fear was lifted.

So however dark your situation, don't give up hope. There is life, there is strength, there is refreshing power awaiting you from the hand of God. You can find the light of a new day as you turn to Him in simple faith and say, in the words of W. H. Doane's hymn, "Pass Me Not," "Heal my wounded, broken spirit." He can, and He will!

CHAPTER 3

Turn Out the Lights, the Party's Over:
THE LAST BABYLONIAN BASH

It was author Robert Louis Stevenson who said, "Everyone sooner or later sits down to a banquet of consequences."

For the late baseball Hall of Famer Mickey Mantle, that regret-filled banquet began in 1994, when Mantle faced up to his forty-two-year addiction to alcohol and checked himself into a rehabilitation center. He completed the program successfully, but along with that success came the realization of what his "fast lane" style of living had cost him and his family.

Mantle acknowledged, for instance, that he had contributed to the alcohol problems of several of his four sons, one of whom had preceded him at the same rehabilitation center. And he felt remorse at not being a better husband and father.

Mantle also indicated that he felt partly responsible for the death of his son, Billy, who died several years before of Hodgkin's disease, a tragic illness that had killed several generations of Mantle men by the age of forty. Mantle had always feared he would transmit the disease to his sons. Billy's illness was the realization of those fears.

Then in the summer of 1995, doctors discovered that cancer had destroyed Mickey Mantle's liver. As he entered Baylor Hospital in Dallas for a liver transplant, he told the young people of America, "Don't follow my example. I'm no role model." The years of abuse to that magnificent athletic body were about to take their final toll.

Now this is not the end of Mickey Mantle's story, as we will see in a later chapter. But even though there's more to tell, this man's life is a classic illustration of the truth of Stevenson's observation.

As we talk about the great night scenes of the Bible, we are going to visit another "banquet of consequences," described for us in Daniel 5. We are going to read about a night when God turned out the lights on a party and plunged a pleasure-seeking king and his kingdom into darkness.

The story of Belshazzar carries with it a lesson we need to read and heed as believers, and a warning that we plead God will burn into the heart of America.

Let's set the scene: "Belshazzar the king made a great feast for a thousand of his lords, and drank wine in the presence of the thousand" (Dan. 5:1).

A Drunken Party

Belshazzar was the powerful king of Babylon, the grandson of Babylon's most famous king, Nebuchadnezzar. Belshazzar was the ultimate party animal. He apparently loved pleasure and lived for pleasure. It was obvious he had not learned, as his famous grandfather had learned, that every day he lived, every breath he took, was from God Almighty.

So in his arrogance, Belshazzar threw a party that became a nightmare because God crashed it. I want you to think about this party for a few moments. The Bible says it was a night of revelry, an orgy of drunkenness. One thousand of Belshazzar's lords were in attendance at this party, along with many other people.

They were having a great time. Indeed, the Scripture says there is pleasure in sin. We make a mistake if we tell people there is no pleasure in sin. But the problem with sin's pleasures, according to Hebrews 11:25, is that they are "passing pleasures." They are temporary. They don't last. That means there will always be a morning after the night before.

So this bash was in full swing when Belshazzar crossed the line. The king "gave the command to bring the gold and silver vessels which his father Nebuchadnezzar had taken from the temple which had been in Jerusalem, that the king and his lords, his wives, and his concubines might drink from them" (Dan. 5:2).

Belshazzar decided he wanted to drink from the sacred vessels that had been brought from the temple in Jerusalem when Nebuchadnezzar sacked Jerusalem and took the Jews captive. Back in Jerusalem, in the Holy Place, those vessels had been dedicated to God's service. Now they would be used in this drunken orgy.

In their sinful and foolish pleasure, Belshazzar and his fellow party animals crossed the line and said good-bye to the grace of God. God moved into that banquet hall, judgment fell, and the lights went out.

That very night, as Belshazzar and all of his lords and ladies blasphemed God in drunken debauchery, the Medes and the Persians dammed up the river running through

Babylon, entered the city via the dry riverbed, killed Belshazzar, and overthrew his kingdom (Dan. 5:30–31). The party was over!

Paying the Consequences

Belshazzar paid the ultimate price because he failed to learn this vital lesson: The breath we have and the life we've been given are an opportunity to live for God, to glorify Him, to obey Him. You can either invest your life for His glory or you can spend your life living for yourself.

Now, the Bible is clear. We are accountable for our actions. And while it is possible for an individual to rebel against God, to determine to sin, and in prideful disdain even shake a fist in the face of Almighty God, we need to remember that our lives are being weighed. We are being judged every day.

I know it's not socially acceptable or politically correct today to speak of the judgment of God. But the fact is, our God is a God of judgment and righteousness. The Scripture says, "For You are not a God who takes pleasure in wickedness" (Ps. 5:4).

You say, "But aren't you talking about the God of the Old Testament?" No, I'm talking about the God of the Bible. Jesus Himself spoke more of judgment, more of hell, and more of condemnation upon those who reject grace and turn from salvation than He spoke on any other subject in all of His teachings. So it's very important for us to realize that our lives are being weighed by Almighty God.

A Warning to America

Belshazzar and his friends got drunk that night, and in their drunkenness they perpetrated all manner of evil, including praise to their false gods (Dan. 5:3–4). The sailors used to say, "Candy is dandy, but liquor is quicker." That's why I think the message below bears repeating. Some members of Alcoholics Anonymous say:

We drank for happiness and became unhappy.
We drank for joy and became miserable.
We drank for sociability and became argumentative.
We drank for sophistication and became obnoxious.
We drank for friendship and made enemies.
We drank for sleep and awakened without rest.
We drank "medicinally" and acquired health problems.
We drank for relaxation and got the shakes.
We drank for bravery and became afraid.
We drank for confidence and became doubtful.
We drank to make conversation easier and slurred our speech.
We drank to feel heavenly and ended up feeling like hell.
We drank to forget and were forever haunted.
We drank for freedom and became slaves.
We drank to erase problems and saw them multiply.
We drank to cope with life and invited death.

What a message for America today! I'm often asked this question about our country: "Are we going to face the judgment of God?" I believe we're already facing the judgment of God. Just look around us. All God has to do to send judgment is take His hand of blessing and grace from a nation or a people.

As we look at all the problems we're facing politically, socially, and culturally, I think we have to admit that God is withdrawing His presence. I think we have to admit that judgment is falling upon America. Now, I don't believe it's too late. I believe revival can come.

Why? Because God's presence will always be there, just as it was that evil night in Babylon. The psalmist said, "If I make my bed in hell, behold, You are there" (Ps. 139:8).

The Law of Sowing and Reaping

You may think you can run from the face of God or hide from the presence of the Lord. But He is always there, weighing and judging. Those who have turned away from God and are living in disobedience may think they are getting away with it. But as we saw above, the Bible says, "Be sure your sin will find you out" (Num. 32:23). Your sin will chase you down.

There is a law of life that is just as permanent and just as powerful as the law of gravity. It is the law of sowing and reaping. What we sow, we reap. That's true agriculturally. It is also true spiritually. Paul tells us in Galatians 6:7–8:

> Do not be deceived, God is not mocked; for whatever a man sows, that he will also reap. For he who sows to his flesh will of the flesh reap corruption, but he who sows to the Spirit will of the Spirit reap everlasting life.

Some people sow the seeds of sin and then pray for crop failure every Sunday. Somehow they think they can sow seeds of foolish and sinful pleasure and it won't catch up with them. But the harvest will surely come. Your sin will catch up with you. Someday, the lights will go out and the party will be over.

That's exactly what happened to Belshazzar on his night of revelry, debauchery, and drunkenness. This night of sin turned into a night of revelation. Let's go back to Daniel 5 and look at the rest of the story.

The End of Belshazzar's Party

Little did Belshazzar and his fellow party people realize that God was about to serve the last course of the evening. He was about to serve them their just desserts:

In the same hour the fingers of a man's hand appeared and wrote opposite the lampstand on the plaster of the wall of the king's palace; and the king saw the part of the hand that wrote.

(Dan. 5:5)

Suddenly, everything became deathly quiet, a hush settled over the crowd. People gasped in horror as this supernatural phenomenon occurred before their very eyes. Were they seeing things? Were they just drunk and hallucinating?

No, the hand of God was moving in their midst. They could see, and perhaps even hear, a scratching noise on the plaster.

Belshazzar and his guests sobered up in a hurry. Belshazzar was scared to death, so frightened that the Scripture says his knees were knocking (Dan. 5:6). His liver had a quiver! He was terrified because he realized something frightening was happening.

These fingers wrote an inscription, as we're told later (Dan. 5:25), but no one knew what the words meant. So in verse 7, we're told that Belshazzar called for "the astrologers, the Chaldeans, and the soothsayers," the intelligentsia of his kingdom, to interpret the handwriting. They all came and scratched their heads because they couldn't figure out what the words meant.

Someone finally told the king, "There's a man by the name of Daniel who's been around this kingdom a long time. Why, Belshazzar, he knew your grandfather Nebuchadnezzar. And he's been known to interpret dreams and to speak of the supernatural." So they found Daniel.

Notice that Daniel, who was now an older man and a high official in the kingdom, was not at that party. He had wisely absented himself from that debauched affair. And as a result of not being there and participating in that sin, Daniel now had a witness opportunity. He had an opportunity to step in and bring the Word of God because they were look-ing for a man with a message, a man who could interpret the inscription.

So Daniel came with a very simple message: Turn out the lights, the party's over. First, he gave Belshazzar a history les-son the king should not have forgotten (Dan. 5:18–21).

These verses recount how God humbled Nebuchadnezzar by afflicting him with insanity until Nebuchadnezzar learned this truth: "The Most High God rules in the kingdom of men, and appoints over it whomever He chooses" (Dan. 5:21).

Go back to Daniel 4:28–37 and read the story for your-self. Nebuchadnezzar lost his mind and became like a wild animal, his fingernails growing long, and his beard and hair becoming matted and covering his body. He lived among the animals.

But then Nebuchadnezzar had a radical conversion expe-rience. God gave him a second chance, and Nebuchadnezzar believed in the God of heaven (Dan. 4:34–37).

Daniel reminded Belshazzar of this and said, "Belshazzar, [you] have not humbled your heart, although you knew all this. And you have lifted yourself up against the Lord of heaven" (Dan. 5:22–23a). Now notice the last part of verse 23, where Daniel continues, "the God who holds your breath in His hand and owns all your ways, you have not glorified."

Daniel is utterly fearless and forthright here. Think about it. You are called in to bring a message to the king. In those days, if the king didn't like your message, he could have your head in an instant. But old Daniel was so gritty that even the lions didn't want to chew on him. He was strong for the Lord.

Daniel stood before that king and said it exactly the way it needed to be said. He didn't back up, let up, or shut up until the king had heard God's message: "Belshazzar, you've missed it. You've lived for pleasure. You've lived for sin. You've lived for yourself. And you have dishonored the very God who gives you breath. You had a chance. You knew better, Belshazzar!"

So Daniel read the sobering inscription: "MENE, MENE, TEKEL, UPHARSIN" (Dan. 5:25). Then he interpreted it: "God has numbered your kingdom, and finished it. . . . You have been weighed in the balances, and found wanting. . . . Your Kingdom has been divided, and given to the Medes and Persians" (Dan. 5:26–28).

Belshazzar was so impressed that he heaped honor upon Daniel—an attempt, I think, to try and appease God by applauding His servant. But it was too late. The party was already over. It was the last thing Belshazzar ever did, for "that very night Belshazzar, king of the Chaldeans, was slain" (Dan. 5:29–30).

Lessons We Need to Learn

What a sobering account. There are a lot of lessons we can draw from this portion of Scripture as individual Christians and even as Americans. Let me highlight a few.

The first concerns the consternation of the king's counselors. The picture of them standing there in utter bewilderment reminds me of the intelligentsia of our own day, those "experts" who reject the Word and the warnings of God and then cannot interpret the activity of God. They can only scratch their heads in wonder at what's happening in our society.

A second lesson I see here concerns you and me as believers. Just as Daniel refused to take part in Belshazzar's drunken, God-dishonoring party, there are times in our lives as followers of the Lord Jesus Christ when we must refuse to participate for social reasons or in any other situation with those who do not know God. Then when the time comes for a witness, we're ready.

Notice also that God had numbered the days of Belshazzar's kingdom. God has numbered our days too. The psalmist said in Psalm 90:12, "Teach us to number our days, / That we may gain a heart of wisdom." We need to use our days wisely, because we won't live forever. Are you numbering your days? We count years as birthdays, but God counts days.

Why is it so important to number our days? Because when our number is up, the Scripture says, "It is appointed for men to die once, but after this the judgment" (Heb.

9:27). No matter how much you jog or how you eat, you cannot escape God's judgment.

You can improve the quality of your life, but you u. add one day to its length. You are in the hand of God. Belshazzar had no idea that night that he was going to die and wake up in the presence of a holy God. But he did.

God also told Belshazzar that he had been "weighed in the balances, and found wanting." Belshazzar was a spiritual and moral lightweight and his kingdom was finished because there was no repentance. He was warned, but he refused to repent. Therefore, the judgment fell.

Listen to Proverbs 29:1: "He who is often rebuked, and hardens his neck, / Will suddenly be destroyed, and that without remedy." Just like that, Belshazzar's life was over. Right in the middle of one of the most pleasurable nights of his life, God turned out the lights. The party was over. There was no remedy, and this debauched king stood face-to-face in judgment and condemnation before a holy God.

A Necessary Message

One Sunday morning I preached a hard-hitting, straight-forward message from the Gospel of Mark on the unpardonable sin, the sin of saying no to God so often that His Spirit ceases to strive and to bring conviction of sin.

In that message I told how there comes a point in a person's life that if he rejects Christ, he sins against the Holy Spirit and the Spirit simply withdraws the attractive, alluring presence of Christ from that person's life and there's no more opportunity to be saved. I showed from the Bible that this is the damning sin of Scripture, the only sin that cannot be forgiven.

In the congregation that morning was a young man named George. He was shaken and moved by the message because he realized that it was possible for him to say no to God one last time. He didn't sleep all that night.

The next day, George was still so shaken that he picked up the phone in his car and called a friend who knew Jesus, just as Belshazzar called for Daniel. Driving down the interstate, George asked his friend, "How do I become a Christian?" And right there on the mobile phone, his friend led George to faith in Jesus.

Later, I had the privilege of performing the marriage ceremony for George and his lovely bride as they committed themselves before God to Him and to each other to establish a Christian marriage and a Christian home.

The judgment of God is real. God judges sin. Don't think that you can get by with your sin. There are Christians who think, "Oh, I'm saved. I'm going to go to heaven. I can live a substandard Christian life, be a second-class citizen of the kingdom, do it my way, and get away with it by the grace of God."

You'll *not* get away with it, because God will discipline His children. God will judge His own—not to condemn a Christian to hell, because that can't happen. But Christians will receive discipline from the hand of God.

In other words, if you sin and think you are getting away with it, you are either headed for hell or for the woodshed. If you're not saved, you're headed for hell. But if you are a child of God, then you are headed for the woodshed because God's going to discipline you, and it is going to be severe if you persist in disobeying Him.

However, if you say yes to Jesus Christ, you can be forgiven. The God who holds your breath in His hands, the God who is numbering your days, the God who is weighing your life, is waiting for you to come to Him in repentance and faith.

Please don't think, "Well, I'll live a good life. I'll do the best that I can. I'll go to church. And when I fail, I'll promise to do better."

It won't ever add up! It will never tip the scales. If you try to make it on your own, you will be weighed and found wanting in the sight of a holy God. The lights will surely go out, and your party will be over.

The only way to be saved is to trust in the One who died for your sins and rose again that you might be forgiven. Then when you stand before God it will not be in judgment, because you'll stand before Him clothed in the righteousness of Jesus Christ.

If you don't know Christ, run to Him today . . . before the lights go out. And if you're a Christian who needs to repent and return to the Lord, come back to Him today . . . before the party's over.

CHAPTER 4

Night Light:
DANIEL AND THE LIONS

During a recent trip to Israel, I experienced one of the most moving, stunning sights I have ever seen.

My wife, Deb, and I were at the museum in Jerusalem dedicated to the Jewish victims of the Nazi Holocaust. At the memorial to the two million children who perished at Hitler's hands, I walked down a long, dark, labyrinthine tunnel. Funeral dirges were playing in the background, interspersed with sounds of people moaning in deep agony and grief.

As I walked along that path, my eyes became accustomed to the darkness. That is by plan of the memorial's designers, of course, because at the end of this tunnel the visitor steps into a small room with a single candle burning on a table.

The sight of this lone candle glowing in the darkness was riveting enough. But what stunned me was that through the use of mirrors, the candle's flame became literally hundreds of thousands of points of reflected light, each light representing a child who died in the Holocaust.

As I stood there overwhelmed by this sight, a recorded voice started reading the names of these children in Hebrew. In fact, our guide told us that there was one point of light in that room for each child who died.

The guide also reminded us that this museum and memorial were built not only to commemorate the dead, but to underscore the vow Israel and the Jewish people made to themselves concerning the Holocaust: "Never again."

For the Jewish people, that vow speaks of the strength of character that Israel has found to go on and survive as a nation, a strength forged in the fires of Nazi ovens. Throughout Israel's history, God has preserved His chosen people—sometimes *from* the fire, and other times *through* the fire.

The night scene we are about to consider did not involve a literal fire, but it was as fiery a trial as any biblical character was called upon to endure. I am talking about the night the prophet Daniel spent in a den of lions.

Daniel in the lions' den must surely rank in the top ten of the most familiar and beloved Bible stories. But this remarkable account is about much more than God taming a pack of fierce lions. It reveals the faith of a great man of God, and the power of God to preserve His people.

The Personality of Daniel

Now we just dealt with Daniel in the preceding chapter. So why are we discussing him again? I can think of at least two reasons. The first reason is the reason I just mentioned. The account of Daniel in the den of lions is one of the great night scenes of the Bible. This book would be incomplete without it.

The second reason is the man Daniel himself. He is one of the most remarkable saints in all of the Bible. His faithfulness to God over many decades and through two major pagan empires is unparalleled. We could spend a lot of time learning spiritual lessons from this hero of the faith. Two chapters in any book are not too much space to give him.

So with all of that in mind, let's set the stage for the drama we are going to read about in chapter 6 of the book of Daniel. By now Daniel was close to ninety years of age. He had survived the fall of the Babylonian kingdom to the Medes and Persians (Dan. 5).

Daniel had in fact prospered through this major change in world powers. So much so that, according to Daniel 6:1–3, he was one of three top "governors" or administrators appointed by King Darius to oversee the great Persian kingdom. And not surprisingly, Daniel soon "distinguished himself above the [other] governors" (v. 3).

If any man had stood the test of time and trial, it was Daniel. He had been taken to Babylon as a teenage Jewish captive. There he purposed not to defile himself, but to maintain his integrity. The Lord honored Daniel's faithfulness, and he served the kings of Babylon for many years without compromising his testimony.

They could change this man's homeland. They could change his language. They could change his education. They could change his name. They could change the pagan kingdom he was called to serve. But they could not change Daniel's heart. He was a man of resolute purpose, and through all the changes he never changed. He was the same man at ninety that he was at nineteen.

The Plot Against Daniel

After Daniel's promotion by Darius, jealousy reared its ugly head. The other two governors and the 120 lesser politicians within the Persian government decided that

Daniel had to go (Dan. 6:4). They scratched around like a pack of weasels, trying to find something wrong with Daniel's service so they could blow the whistle and do away with him.

They hadn't counted on Daniel's spotless character. They soon realized that there was nothing in the character and personality of Daniel they could capitalize on. So they hatched a scheme right out of hell to try and bring Daniel down. They would attack him at the point of his faith.

Envy is a terrible thing. Someone has said that envy is the tribute failure pays to success. If that's true, then these Persian politicos were paying high tribute to Daniel, because they were consumed with envy.

Their evil plan was finally set in motion not because there was a flaw in Daniel, but because there was a flaw in Darius. His flaw was his pride. These men gathered themselves around his throne and said:

> *King Darius, live forever! All the governors of the kingdom, the administrators and satraps, the counselors and advisors, have consulted together to establish a royal statute and to make a firm decree, that whoever petitions any god or man for thirty days, except you, O king, shall be cast into the den of lions.*
>
> (Dan. 6:6b–7)

Back in the fifties there was a TV show called "Queen for a Day." These men proposed to Darius that he declare himself "God for a Month." Darius liked the sound of that, so in his pride he signed the unchangeable decree that would doom Daniel to the lions' den (Dan. 6:8–9).

The Prayer Life of Daniel

There was method in these men's demonic madness, because they knew Daniel would pray to the one true God just as he had always prayed, decree or no decree. In fact, they went running from the king's presence straight to Daniel's house so they could catch him in the act of defying the king's order. They were not to be disappointed.

Daniel was faced with a decision: to pray to his God and maintain his faith and integrity, or to acquiesce to the "God of the Month" plan. Now Daniel could have rationalized like many of us tend to rationalize our decisions when the going gets tough.

Daniel could have said, "Well, after all it's just thirty days. If I don't pray for thirty days, I'm still a believer. The Lord knows my heart."

Or he could have reasoned, "Look, who says I have to pray publicly? I'll continue my custom of praying in my chamber on my knees, but I'll just shut the windows. God hears me when I pray secretly just as well as when I pray publicly. I don't want these people to think I'm some kind of religious show-off."

Daniel could also have argued, "Maybe I just need to back off a little here. If I pray publicly, I'll get tossed in the lions' den. I'll lose my testimony. I'll lose my place of influence in the government that God has given me, to say nothing of my life. All the good I've been able to accomplish over all these years will be lost if I disobey and pray."

Daniel could have done a lot of things, but Daniel 6:10 tells us what he actually did. He went home, opened his windows toward Jerusalem, and knelt down to pray and give thanks to God. And he did it not once, but three times, "as was his custom since early days" (v. 10). Daniel had been doing this for about seventy years. He wasn't about to quit now.

One day I saw a sign in a man's office that said, "If you're having an especially busy day, skip your devotions. Signed, Satan." Daniel understood the importance of maintaining his devotion to God. He refused to skip his prayer life simply because his earthly boss made a rule against it.

Now we're not even to our night scene yet, but we can already begin drawing valuable lessons for our spiritual lives from this story. Notice several things about Daniel's prayer life from verse 10.

First, Daniel had a *place* for prayer, an upper room where he constantly prayed. Isn't it interesting that Jesus chose an upper room for His last night of intimate fellowship with His disciples (Mark 14:15)?

Second, Daniel had a *posture* in prayer. He knelt as a symbol of his surrender and yieldedness to God. You can pray in any position, but Daniel assumed the posture of submission when he prayed.

Third, Daniel prayed according to a set *period*, three times every day.

Fourth, Daniel prayed with a clear *prospect* in mind. The Scripture says he prayed with his windows opened toward Jerusalem. Remember, Daniel was an exile in Babylon. But to show that he believed in God's promise that He would one day bring His people back to the land of promise, Daniel prayed before an open window with his face toward Jerusalem.

As the light poured in, the glory of God filled Daniel's soul and the fresh air of the Holy Spirit moved in his heart as day after day he looked to the Lord and offered thanks-giving and praise through prayer.

Make no mistake about it, however. Even though the sun shone as Daniel prayed, this was a dark day for him. He prayed under a death threat, and I believe he knew that his enemies would be spying on him that day as he prayed (Dan. 6:11).

Let me tell you a secret to surviving your dark days. It will explain why Daniel prayed even in the face of death, and why you and I need to become people of prayer no matter what.

Here's the secret: What we are in the darkness in prayer is what we really are. The rest of it is just religious talk. As I said in the Introduction, character is made in the dark. A Christian is like a photograph. There must be a period in the darkness before we can be released into the light.

Daniel had light in his soul because he prayed. The glow of God was upon him because he prayed. Prayer was the secret of his life. It was the secret of his courage, his convic-tion, his commitment. His outward life was simply the expression of an inward life of prayer.

Daniel knew he was in the Lord's hands, so he kept on praying. If you can kneel before God, you can stand before any man. That's what Daniel did.

The Preservation of Daniel

In Daniel 6:11–13 we read that Daniel's enemies acted exactly according to their evil character and their evil plot. They caught him in the act of praying, and ran to King Darius with their news like a bunch of tattletales running to the teacher in the school yard.

Verse 14 makes it clear that even though Daniel was the one caught in this plot, Darius was the one trapped by it. He realized he had been trapped by his own pride. It dawned on him that he had been set up by the men standing before him.

It did not matter, however. The law of the Medes and Persians could not be altered. Even though Darius cared for Daniel, and even though he would be losing his best administrator, he had no choice but to carry out the sentence on Daniel.

Now Darius stalled for as long as he possibly could (Dan. 6:14b) while he checked every legal loophole. But in verse 15, the plotters came to him and said in so many words, "Come on, O king. Quit stalling. You know how this works. You know what you have to do."

So with a heavy heart, King Darius gave the order and they threw Daniel into the den of lions that evening. This would have been an intensely dark place, because this den was probably an abandoned cistern in which hungry lions were kept for executions.

These cisterns were customarily sealed with a heavy stone, so Daniel would have been at the bottom of a deep well with no light whatsoever to break up the darkness.

Before they sealed the den, Darius said to Daniel, "Your God, whom you serve continually, He will deliver you" (Dan. 6:16b). Those are the last words Daniel heard before the stone slid into place and the den fell dark (Dan. 6:17).

Now Darius didn't know it, but he was a prophet that night. God did deliver Daniel. The scene here is amusing to me, for it was the king safe in his palace who was restless and fearful, not Daniel in the lions' den (Dan. 6:18). It was the king who couldn't sleep. There were no dancing girls and no entertainment for Darius that night. He was up fretting all night.

In my imagination I can picture Daniel relaxing just a bit as the lions cease their roaring. It's cold in that dark, damp hole, but about that time a lioness and her cubs walk up and snuggle up next to Daniel to provide warmth. Then the head lion of the den comes over and lies down at Daniel's feet. Daniel falls asleep and sleeps like a baby.

The text describes what happened the next day: "Then the king arose very early in the morning and went in haste to the den of lions" (Dan. 6:19). Darius didn't need an alarm clock to stir him awake that morning. He had just suffered through the longest night of his life.

When he got to the den, Darius shouted out the question he had been waiting all night to ask: "Daniel, servant of the living God, has your God, whom you serve continually, been able to deliver you from the lions?" (Dan. 6:20b).

Imagine the king's relief when the prophet called back, "O king, live forever! My God sent His angel and shut the lions' mouths, so that they have not hurt me, because I was found innocent before Him; and also, O king, I have done no wrong before you" (Dan. 6:21–22). They hauled Daniel up, and he came out without so much as a scratch (Dan. 6:23).

Daniel was delivered that night because he believed in his God. He was delivered from the darkness of the den because he trusted in God, and God has preserved Daniel's experience for us in His Word as a reminder that He can preserve us.

There is etched on my mind a painting of Daniel in the lions' den I remember seeing as a child. Daniel is standing there as the lions circle him and begin moving in closer. Daniel is looking up, and a beam of light is shining down from above on his face as he focuses, not on the lions, but on the Lord.

Daniel is a supreme example to us that in every circumstance in life, God is faithful. The only thing at issue is whether we will be found faithful to Him. If we will trust Him, we can be prepared to face the darkness of our own lions' den.

Preparing for the Dark Times

So often when we are plunged into the darkness, we are not prepared. The phone call comes, and it's bad news. The doctor's report is in, and there isn't much hope. Suddenly we are plunged into the midst of problems we never imagined.

It is so important, therefore, that while we are in the light, we learn and grow and build spiritual strength so that when the darkness comes, we will not doubt in the darkness what God showed us in the light.

So we need to ask, what does it take to be a Daniel when things have turned against you and you can hear the lions roaring in the distance? A closer look at Daniel's life will reveal some qualities that are vital preparation for surviving the dark nights in our lives.

An "Excellent Spirit"

The first quality I want you to see is that Daniel had an "excellent spirit" (Dan. 6:3). The commentators point out that this was more than just a positive, commendable spirit, although Daniel certainly had that.

The idea here is that Daniel had a real capability for his work. He was qualified in every way, and his life and service were characterized by excellence. That's what made him stand above the rest in whatever he did.

Now Daniel did indeed have a positive spirit. We've already reviewed the adverse things that happened to him. But we never read a complaint coming from Daniel's mouth. His attitude was always inspirational and uplifting. Remember this old saying? "It's not your aptitude, but your attitude that determines your altitude." Daniel soared because he had a sweet spirit.

Nobody enjoys being around someone who's negative and critical and complaining and constantly finding fault. I don't. Those kind of people drain me. They discourage me.

Daniel prospered in a pagan land even among his adversaries. The Scripture says, "When a man's ways please the LORD, / He makes even his enemies to be at peace with him" (Prov. 16:7). Daniel had such an excellent spirit about him that even his enemies desired to promote him. And what about those enemies who refused to "be at peace" with Daniel? Read verse 24 of Daniel 6 and you'll see how God dealt with them.

Let me draw another lesson for us from the example of Daniel's spirit. We live in a dark generation in which we are deeply concerned about the direction our nation is taking. It is right and good that we as Christians take a stand against the sin in our society. But as we do, we must make sure that our attitude stays positive and hopeful and loving and kind.

I'm afraid that many times we Christians have offended and put off the very people we are trying to reach. That's why it's dangerous to so overtly politicize and opinionize the church of Jesus Christ that we find ourselves over in a corner talking only to ourselves. We must make sure that in taking our moral and biblical stand, we do not ostracize and alienate the people we are trying to reach with the gospel.

Daniel worked within first the Babylonian and then the Persian system. That doesn't mean he compromised his faith or ignored sin. We know that's not true. But because of his strong, positive, and excellent spirit, he was able to bring a godly influence to bear upon the kings of two great empires.

Diligence

Daniel's life was also characterized by diligence. He was faithful. He worked hard. He was trustworthy. He performed the duties of his job diligently.

Wherever you work, as a follower of the Lord Jesus Christ you ought to be the best worker, the most faithful man or woman there. You ought to be a person of integrity and credibility, serving diligently and doing all things well.

Tom Landry, the former coach of the Dallas Cowboys, said, "Some kind of excellence is within the reach of every one of us." We have a motto at our church in Dallas that simply says, "Excellence in all things and all things to the glory of God."

Purity

Daniel was also a pure man. Those who thought they could uncover some dirt on him came up empty. He was clean. Even a small army of political weasels, Watergate-type individuals, couldn't find anything on Daniel. They looked everywhere and couldn't find a thing wrong with his character.

This is a convicting thought for all of us, but think about what would happen if somebody put a private investigator on you, watching you day and night. What if a professional investigator or a skilled group of Washington "dirt-diggers" scoured your private world, going through your closet or your checkbook, pulling your income tax return? Would they find integrity, a clean slate?

Daniel's enemies found that kind of integrity and purity in him. He was a blameless man. Now he wasn't perfect. He wasn't sinless. The Bible never intended to portray him like that.

Daniel is the only person other than Joseph in the Old Testament of whom nothing bad is recorded. It's all positive. Nothing is ever said about sin in his life. He sinned, but he was a blameless man. That is the way to live. When you live with integrity, you don't face a guilty conscience.

I heard about a couple in Los Angeles who drove to a fast-food chicken restaurant. The man went in and ordered a bucket of chicken for a picnic they were going to have together. He got his bucket of chicken, got in the car, and drove off—only to discover down the road that the bucket was full of money.

The man realized something was wrong, and that he couldn't keep the money. So he drove back to the chicken restaurant and told the manager, "Sir, I must have been given the wrong bucket by mistake. This bucket is full of money and I want to return it."

The manager said, "Oh, my goodness! These are our day's receipts. We put them in a chicken bucket to disguise them when we take the money to the bank. You must be the last honest man in Los Angeles! People need to know about this. I'm going to call the newspaper and have them send out a reporter and a photographer. Have your wife come in and we'll get a picture of you both for the newspaper. This is a great story."

The man said, "Oh, no, I can't do that!"

The manager said, "Why not?"

The man said, "The woman in the car is not my wife."

Many people look honest on the surface. Many appear to be full of integrity, when on the inside, in the private world, there is sinfulness. But Daniel would have had no reason to fear having his picture in the newspaper.

Spiritual Depth

Finally, I want you to see that Daniel was a deeply spiritual, deeply devoted man. We know he was a man of prayer. I believe his spirituality even made a difference physically for Daniel. He was ninety years of age and still vigorous, still able to serve and excel in the government of Persia.

The apostle John wrote to Gaius, "Beloved, I pray that you may prosper in all things and be in health, just as your soul prospers" (3 John 2). Daniel prospered spiritually and physically. Your body has to age, but you don't have to grow old and calcified in your spirit. Your arteries may harden, but your attitudes should never harden. Even in the later stages of his life, Daniel was strong and vibrant in spirit and body.

The Certainty of the Lions' Den

Daniel was prepared for whatever crisis might come. And the crisis did come in the form of persecution for his success and his faith. There is a price to pay for godly success. Daniel paid that price. His enemies despised his godly character.

Have you discovered that when you live for Jesus Christ, when you stand strong and true and faithful, there will always be those who resent your faith, revile your purity, and despise your morality? Paul wrote, "All who desire to live godly in Christ Jesus will suffer persecution" (2 Tim. 3:12).

Now if you have never taken some heat for being a Christian, if you've never faced some fire and flak because you are a believer in the Lord Jesus Christ, one of two things is true. Either you're not living for Christ in sincerity, or you are off in a "holy hole" somewhere not relating to the world.

But if you stand true and firm and strong for Jesus Christ in your school, at your university, in the marketplace, and in your neighborhood, you will suffer persecution.

The philosopher Plato said that if truth came down from heaven, it would be found so desirable that men would fall down and worship it. But Plato was wrong, for Truth did come down from heaven in the person of Jesus Christ, who said, "I am the way, the truth, and the life" (John 14:6). And when Truth came down from heaven, many didn't worship. Instead, they nailed Truth to a cross. And just as Daniel was delivered to the lions' den out of envy, Jesus Christ was crucified out of envy.

Maybe you're in a lions' den right now. It could be a den of a broken marriage or a broken family. It could be a den of illness or business loss. It could be that someone is slandering you. It could be a satanic attack, for the apostle Peter tells us, "your adversary the devil walks about like a roaring lion, seeking whom he may devour" (1 Peter 5:8).

But even if you are in the darkness of a den of lions, if you will look to God, trust in Him, and rest in Him, you will find strength and help. The trials will come, but they can never ultimately harm us because we are immortal in the will of God.

James put it this way: "Blessed is the man who endures temptation [or trial]; for when he has been approved, he will receive the crown of life which the Lord has promised to those who love Him" (James 1:12).

Our Lord Jesus Christ has defeated the roaring lion, Satan. The battle is already won. If your faith and your hope are in the Lion of the tribe of Judah, even when you face the dark night of your soul, you will find help and deliverance. A little girl in Sunday school said, "The lions didn't eat Daniel because the Lion of the tribe of Judah was in there with him." That was a little girl who knew her Bible.

Daniel was not only lifted up out of that lions' den. King Darius issued a new decree, proclaiming Daniel's God as the God of the Persian kingdom (Dan. 6:25–27). When an unbelieving world observes faith like the faith of a Daniel, many will believe in our God and put their trust in Him.

The Scripture says we are "kept by the power of God" (1 Peter 1:5). We are in the grip of an all-powerful God, and as long as He has a purpose for us here and now, we will live.

That is why I say we are immortal within the will of God. John wrote, "He who does the will of God abides forever" (1 John 2:17). God's plan for Daniel did not include being eaten by lions that dark night, so he wasn't eaten. It's that simple.

And the wonderful thing about being a Christian is that even if we do get eaten by the lions, even if we do lose our lives, we still win because heaven awaits us.

When God wants to take you to heaven, there to serve Him through the ages, He will take you. But until then, He will keep you. Until then, "No weapon formed against you shall prosper" (Isa. 54:17)—including the teeth of lions!

CHAPTER 5

A Different Kind of Darkness:
THE SAGA OF JONAH

I suspect that years from now, many Americans will be able to recall exactly where they were and what they were doing when they first heard the news about the tragic bombing in Oklahoma City on April 19, 1995.

This was one of those events that marks a generation, the way my generation was forever marked by the assassination of President John Kennedy on November 22, 1963.

One of the most poignant stories that came out of Oklahoma City in the hours after the bombing was told by rescuers who had to leave victims trapped in the rubble because of the fear that another bomb was about to explode.

I will never forget the man who told of being by the side of a young woman pinned in the wreckage of the Murrah Federal Building. As word came for the rescuers to leave immediately and run to safety, this man reported how the terror-stricken woman pleaded not to be left alone. He said he could hear her screams as he was forced to leave her alone for a while in her steel-and-concrete prison. Other rescuers reported similar experiences.

It was about forty-five minutes before the second bomb scare was over and rescuers were allowed to return to the victims. In that agonizing period, that young woman probably felt that she was being abandoned to die alone as her pleas for help fell on deaf ears in the eerie silence that often follows an explosion.

Without trying to push the analogy too far, I have to wonder if the prophet Jonah did not feel that he, too, was being abandoned to die as the great fish swallowed him whole. The bars of Jonah's "prison" were not made of steel and concrete, but of bone as his body became lodged in the fish's stomach.

What Jonah tells us is that there is no darkness on earth as horrifying as the darkness in the belly of a great beast. But just as the cries of that young woman were heard and her life was spared, so Jonah's cries from the belly of the beast were heard. In fact, God had been waiting for some time to hear from His rebellious prophet.

The Fleeing Prophet

Talk about suffocating darkness. Talk about God getting your attention. The story of Jonah has all of that, and more. Let's begin unfolding the drama: "Now the word of the LORD came to Jonah the son of Amittai, saying, 'Arise, go to Nineveh, that great city, and cry out against it; for their wickedness has come up before Me'" (Jonah 1:1–2).

The divine directive was clear enough. It contained all the essentials: the who, what, where, and why of Jonah's assignment. But the Bible tells us Jonah "arose to flee to Tarshish from the presence of the LORD. He went down to Joppa, and found a ship going to Tarshish; so he paid the fare, and went down into it, to go with them to Tarshish from the presence of the LORD" (v. 3).

Now we know Jonah was headed for trouble because he was trying to run from God. But at least we can say this much for Jonah at the outset. When God spoke, Jonah was listening. The problem was that Jonah didn't like what he heard. What he heard was God's specific call to get up, go to Nineveh, and warn its people of God's impending judgment.

An Unpopular Message

Why didn't Jonah want to go to Nineveh? Because Nineveh was the capital of the Assyrian empire, the cruel and hated enemies of God's people in Israel. Nineveh was an important and powerful city, full of Gentiles—card-carrying pagans, idol worshipers, the kind of people the God of Israel couldn't possibly care about, or could He?

That was Jonah's question. It knocked him off his feet to think that God could love those "Gentile dogs." He couldn't imagine why God would send him to Nineveh, especially with a message of repentance and salvation.

God was telling Jonah, "I want you, a Jew, to go to Nineveh and stand right in the midst of all those Gentile pagans. And I want you to cry out My message of warning." Jonah knew that would not be a popular message. Who wants to hear that his city is going to be destroyed unless he repents?

So Jonah was called by God to go to an unpopular place and deliver an unpopular message. He had to be thinking, *Why me? Why now?*

The simple fact is that Jonah did not want to go to Nineveh and warn the people of God's judgment because he was afraid they would repent and be preserved. He wanted to see Nineveh and all its people go up in the smoke of God's wrath. Therefore, he figured no prophet, no message. No message, no possibility of repentance.

The Flight to Tarshish

So verse 3 tells us that Jonah became what my parents used to call "bucky." He thought he could outsmart and outrun God. Nineveh was about five hundred miles east of Israel, but Jonah arose and headed for Tarshish, some two thousand miles to the west. He was determined to flee from the presence and the plan of God. Jonah must have known it was a futile effort, but he tried it anyway.

The language of verse 3 is insightful here: "He went down to Joppa . . . [he] went down into [the ship]." The spiral of disobedience is always downward. Jonah went down geographically to Joppa, but he went down spiritually into disobedience. Any move away from the will of God is a downward move.

It's sort of like the first time a person tries downhill skiing. If you have ever done that, you know what I'm talking about. After a few runs you think you know what to do. You think you're ready to leave the beginner's slope, so they take you on up to a much steeper and more difficult slope.

But when you get up there and look down for the first time, you start praying for somebody to come and get you. You finally get up enough courage to point your skis downhill, and you push off what feels like the edge of a cliff. There you go, flying straight downhill, and you realize you're out of control.

When you step out of the will of God, it's like skiing off the edge of a cliff, flying straight downhill, totally out of control. Jonah did that when he boarded that ship for Tarshish.

Now the amazing thing about Jonah is that apparently he was content rather than miserable in his disobedience. We learn that later, when the ship's captain had to wake him up in the storm. As far as Jonah was concerned, the issue of Nineveh was settled. He wasn't going anywhere near that place. He had already slept on his decision, so now he just slept.

The Great Storm

This is one reason I believe God sent that great storm to track Jonah down and bring him back (Jonah 1:4). If Jonah were agonizing over his call to Nineveh, if he were more spiritually sensitive, perhaps God would have let him reach Tarshish, dealing with him all along the way.

God knew that if Jonah ever made it to Tarshish he would melt into the crowd and disappear. God would never see him again, so to speak. To forestall His prophet's further "buckiness," God sent a great storm Jonah's way. Jonah was sailing directly into the teeth of God's displeasure, and that's a losing proposition every time.

You can run, but you can't hide from God. The psalmist asked, "Where can I go from Your Spirit? / Or where can I flee from Your presence? / If I ascend into heaven, You are there; / If I make my bed in hell, behold, You are there. / If I take the wings of the morning, / And dwell in the uttermost parts of the sea, / Even there Your hand shall lead me" (Ps. 139:7–10a).

Jonah was about to learn the truth of that last phrase first-hand! He was asleep, but he was in for a rude awakening. He had stretched out and gotten comfortable in his sin. He was snugly warm in his disobedience, trying to forget about God and His call upon his life.

But God was getting ready to jerk the blanket off of His obstinate prophet and make him hit the cold deck. For you see, while Jonah had forgotten God, God had not forgotten Jonah. The "hound of heaven" was hot on his trail.

The remaining verses of Jonah 1 tell the story of the storm God sent out to track Jonah down and bring him back. The pagan sailors on that ship went through an amazing transformation in the process of trying to ride out the storm. They displayed more concern for life and limb, and more spiritual sensitivity, than Jonah. They even became worshipers of the true God!

And no wonder. These hardened and experienced seamen were frightened within an inch of their lives. They started out by crying out to their pagan gods and throwing cargo overboard to lighten the ship. They were fighting for their lives while Jonah was fast asleep in "the lowest parts of the ship" (Jonah 1:5). And this was all his fault!

The End of the Cruise

What a pathetic condition for a child of God to be in: snoring outside the will of God while a storm is going on all around him. People are fearing for their lives, grasping for any spiritual hope. But here is the believer in the true God, the cause of the storm, asleep at the switch.

Finally, when the casting of lots fingered Jonah as the bad guy, he admitted his rebellion against God. Then the sailors asked him for advice (Jonah 1:11).

Jonah knew his westbound cruise was over, so he told them to throw him into the sea. But to their credit, the sailors weren't murderers. They tried rowing harder, but to no avail (Jonah 1:12–13). Notice what happened next:

> *Therefore they cried out to the LORD and said, "We pray, O LORD, please do not let us perish for this man's life, and do not charge us with innocent blood; for You, O LORD, have done as it pleased You."*
>
> (Jonah 1:14)

The scene here is one of complete chaos. God was angry, Jonah was miserable, and the sailors weren't too thrilled either. Everything was backwards. The pagans were calling the believer to account spiritually, and instead of bringing joy, the believer was spreading misery like a virus.

At least the sailors got rid of their misery by tossing Jonah overboard (Jonah 1:15). From now on, this unhappy prophet would have only himself for company.

An Act of Grace

Do you realize that this storm was an act of grace and mercy on God's part? We should thank God for the storms He sends to chase us down when we're out of His will and out of fellowship with Him.

God could just cut us off. God could just let us die in our rebellion. Even worse, God could allow us to waste our lives in oblivion in Tarshish. But He tracks down His children and brings them back to Himself.

God not only sent the storm to get Jonah, but He sent the great fish (Jonah 1:17). The fish kept his appointment by swallowing Jonah. As the fish's mouth closed and Jonah slid down into the horrible darkness of the monster's stomach, he thought it was all over. He thought he would die for sure.

The Fearful Prophet

So in his dark prison, Jonah reached out in prayer to make peace with God. But God wasn't ready yet to take Jonah home to heaven. Like the fish, Jonah also had an appointment to keep—in Nineveh. He wasn't going to get out of obeying God by dying as fish food.

Amazing Grace

The grace of God is so amazing to me. I can understand how a man like Joseph, who had been so faithful to God, could be delivered from the darkness of the pit and the darkness of prison and placed at the pinnacle of power in Egypt. I can understand God doing that.

I can understand God working in the life of a man like Job, who was blameless and upright in his generation. When Job's day of darkness fell so heavily upon him, he blessed God and worshiped. It's not hard for me to understand why God would be moved to deliver Job out of all his troubles.

I can see why God would preserve Daniel through the dark night of Babylon's fall, and then draw him up out of the darkness of the lions' den. After all, Daniel was utterly and unreservedly committed to God his whole life.

Again, I can understand how God would work in the life of Stephen, that faithful deacon who preached the Word of Christ and was stoned to death for it. God granted Stephen the ultimate deliverance, taking him to heaven.

And I can understand why, when faithful believers go through dark days that are no fault of their own, God comes to their aid with His saving and delivering power.

However, it is hard to understand how God could deliver a reprobate and rebellious prophet like Jonah who had wasted his opportunity and rejected his call. But that's what God did. In Jonah's darkest hour, God delivered him. Only the grace of our Lord Jesus Christ can explain that.

Peter also experienced that grace, as we will see in Chapter 8. After he had warmed himself at the fires of those who were about to crucify Jesus, after he had denied his Lord not once, but three times, Peter was plunged into the darkest night of his life. And yet the Lord Jesus restored Peter in His grace.

New Lessons

In the stomach of that great fish, Jonah was about to find out some things about God he had never experienced before, at least not under such drastic circumstances. Now in total misery, with his full attention finally focused on the Lord, "Jonah prayed to the LORD his God from the fish's belly" (Jonah 2:1).

What did Jonah find out? First, he found out that God's presence wasn't limited to Israel, to the confines of the temple in Jerusalem. He was present even in the belly of a fish at the bottom of the sea. On the darkest night of Jonah's life, even when he was out of fellowship with God, he found himself in the presence of God.

More than that, Jonah found out that God's love and grace extend as far as His children can run from Him, and much farther. Jonah may have thought that the fish's belly was the last stop on earth for him, but he found grace in that terribly dark place. Paul put it this way in Romans 5:20: "Where sin abounded, grace abounded much more."

People often ask, "But can't believers fall from grace?" I don't read anything in my Bible about believers falling from grace. All I can find is people falling into grace. We are kept by the power of God.

Jonah was still God's man. And you can't keep God's man down when he turns to Him. Jonah discovered the presence of God in the dark night of his disobedience, in the suffocating darkness of that fish's stomach. If God can meet Jonah there, I don't think you and I ever have to worry about God losing track of us!

You can't outrun the love of God. You can't run far enough to find yourself outside the boundaries of His grace. The song says it so well: "His love has no limit, His grace has no measure, His power has no boundary known unto men; For out of His infinite riches in Jesus, He giveth, and giveth, and giveth again!" (Hubert Mitchell, "He Giveth More Grace," © 1941, Lillenas Publishing Co.).

Please don't misunderstand. God will discipline His disobedient children, even harshly if necessary. If you keep trying to run from Him, He will hobble you if necessary to bring you back. But like a doting Father, He will come to you in love and grace at the first word of your repentance.

Jonah's Repentance

Jonah may not have been a very good sailor, but he would have been a good candidate for the Navigators, the Christian ministry that is famous for emphasizing Scripture memory.

How do I know? Because Jonah's prayer of confession in chapter 2 is full of scriptural thoughts, if not word-for-word quotations. There in his dark prison, Jonah started pulling out every Scripture reference and allusion he could think of to express his heart to the Lord.

Jonah now realized that God knew his name and his address. God knew where he was, so he called out to the Lord in His name, reminding Him of His Word. That is a terrific prayer strategy, by the way.

The imprisoned prophet concluded his prayer this way: "I will sacrifice to You with the voice of thanksgiving; I will pay what I have vowed. Salvation is of the LORD" (Jonah 2:9).

This is a remarkable confession of faith because at this point, Jonah had no clue he was going to be delivered from this different kind of darkness. He didn't know he would be given a second chance. He figured he would die in the fish. But at least he would die with the assurance that his eternal destiny was settled with God.

The Forceful Prophet

In one sense, it would have been easier for Jonah to die inside the fish than to be spit out and asked to start all over again. But that's just what God had in mind for him: "The LORD spoke to the fish, and it vomited Jonah onto dry land" (v. 10).

Now that Jonah was back on dry land, somewhat the worse for wear but ready to obey, God was ready to begin one of the greatest revivals in history (Jonah 3:1–11). And the city of Nineveh responded wholeheartedly to Jonah's message of repentance and judgment.

Everyone, from the king to the cows, repented in sackcloth and ashes. The people turned to the living God, and at least 120,000 were saved.

Who else but God could do so much with a derelict, disobedient prophet? It just goes to show you what He can do with us once we are ready to step out of the darkness into His light.

You have to love the opening line of Jonah 3: "The word of the LORD came to Jonah the second time." Thank God, the darkness doesn't have to be the last word in our lives. Our God is the God of the second chance, and the third chance, and whatever chance you need. He is there to extend His grace to you.

The Frustrated Prophet

I know there is another chapter to the story of Jonah that seems to complicate things, because Jonah went off and pouted over Nineveh's repentance. But Jonah 4 only underscores several of the things we've been talking about all along.

For instance, Jonah 4 underscores the wonderful grace of God. Not only was He gracious to spare Nineveh, but He was gracious to His petulant prophet in not judging him on the spot for his rotten attitude. I'm afraid if you or I were God, we would have lost our patience at that point and Jonah would have been a french fry.

And even though Jonah still had a long way to go, the last chapter of his story does not negate either his repentance or his obedience in going to Nineveh and delivering God's message. All chapter 4 shows is that while God got Jonah out of the darkness, He hadn't yet got all of the darkness out of Jonah. In other words, Jonah was still very much human.

So I'm content to leave Jonah sulking under the boiling sun, because that's where God left him, at least as far as the

Bible is concerned. What happened between God and the prophet after this is their business.

I am not saying that Jonah's attitude doesn't matter. But I think the reason God ended the book of Jonah with a question mark is because He wants us to ask ourselves a hard question rather than try to figure out what God finally did with Jonah.

A Hard Question

Here's the hard question God wants us to ask ourselves: Are we running from what we know to be His will and plan for our lives?

You may say, "Wait a minute, Jack. I thought this book was about the wonderful ways God comes to us in our darkness and lifts us up. This isn't a very comfortable question."

I'll get to the comforting part in a minute. But I don't want to leave you comfortable if you're hiding out from God. Remember that false comfort was part of Jonah's problem. He was so comfortable in his rebellion and sin that he fell fast asleep on that ship. If God hadn't jerked him out of bed, he might still be snoring!

What a picture of so many Christians today, asleep and content outside the will of God! That is what happens when we try to run from God. We become spiritually insensitive. We move away from our responsibilities. We step away from what God has called us to do.

I wonder how many Christians are running from God today. One psychologist observed that you would be hard-pressed to find anyone who hasn't fantasized at least once about chucking it all and running away from his or her responsibilities.

Thankfully, most Christians don't do that. But I wonder how many Christians are constantly on the run, grabbing this or that flight, keeping long hours, to escape the responsibilities of home and family; to keep from being alone with themselves and God because they don't want to do what He has called them to do.

So my question to you is, Are you trying to run away from God? If you are running, you better not get too comfortable. He loves you too much to let you go too far. Jonah proves that we can't escape God's presence no matter how hard or fast we run.

How do you know if you're running from a step of obedience God wants you to take? He will reveal it to you if you will listen. Take time to be still and know that He is God (Ps. 46:10). Be alert to that still small voice like the voice Elijah heard (1 Kings 19:12; see Chapter 2). Meditate in God's Word, and let Him show you His will.

Never Too Late

But you may feel it's too late for you to do that. You may think you've already run too far away from God to come back. Your darkness may be so thick you feel as if you've been swallowed by a great fish and there's no hope.

Does that describe you? Then let me give you a word of comfort and hope. If you will cry out to God in repentance from the belly of your beast, He will hear and answer. For you see, as long as you are still alive and kicking, you haven't run too far for God to give you a second chance. Just ask Roy Riegels about running too far the wrong way and second chances.

If you recognize the name of Roy "Wrong Way" Riegels, you are either a trivia fan or a football fan—or maybe both. Riegels was a member of the University of California football team that met Georgia Tech in the Rose Bowl on New Year's Day, 1929.

In the second quarter of a 0-0 game, Georgia Tech was in its own territory when a Tech running back fumbled. Riegels, playing on the defensive line for California, scooped up the ball at the Tech 35-yard line. He said later that as he took off with the ball, he got shoved and hit and spun around by several would-be tacklers and completely lost his bearings.

The result was that Riegels took off in the wrong direction, straight toward the Georgia Tech goal line. He ran as hard and as fast as he could, only to be stopped by a frantic teammate at the California 3-yard line (had Riegels crossed the goal line, it would have counted as a touchdown for Georgia Tech).

Riegels' teammate tried to turn him around and get him started the right way, but several Georgia Tech players slammed him to the turf at the 3-yard line. Even though it was still California's ball, they were trapped so deep in their own territory that they decided to punt their way out of the trouble.

The teammate who had caught up with Riegels now stood in the end zone to punt, but the kick was blocked and the ball rolled out of the end zone. Georgia Tech was awarded a safety, and those two points proved to be the margin of victory in an eventual 8-7 Tech victory.

Riegels was horrified by his mistake. At halftime in the locker room, the California coach stood up to give his halftime talk. But Riegels was not listening. He sat weeping with a towel over his head, his face buried in his hands. He figured he had gone too far. The coach would never trust him again.

But then he heard the coach announce that the same eleven men who had started the first half would start the second half. That included him. Riegels followed the coach out of the locker room as the players were returning to the field. "Coach, you said the same eleven men would start the second half. You don't mean me too, do you?"

"Yes, Roy, I mean you. Get in there!"

"But, Coach," Riegels protested, "I can't go back in there after what I did."

The coach said, "Yes, you can, Roy. We've got another half to play. I believe in you." Football history records that Roy Riegels went out and played the game of his life.

After the game, a reporter asked Riegels, "How could you play with such heart in the second half after the terrible mistake you made in the first half?"

Riegels is said to have replied, "How could I do any less? My coach believed in me." More than that, Riegels rose above the heartache and humiliation of that moment to forge a successful career as a high school football coach and a member of the armed forces—although he carried the nickname "Wrong Way" the rest of his life.

That's the good news on Roy Riegels. Now here's the good news for you. You may have run in the wrong direction from the presence of the Lord, but the game's only half over. If you will turn around and come back to God, you will find that Jesus has already paid your fare back from Tarshish to Nineveh.

Even though your darkness may be of an altogether different kind from any you have known before, God can rescue you from it just as He rescued Jonah from the belly of the beast. Remember, "Salvation is of the LORD"!

CHAPTER 6

Questions in the Night:
"Night School" for Nicodemus

Back in Chapter 3, I told you about the final days of one of my childhood heroes, Mickey Mantle. He played baseball as well as anyone has ever played it, and he lived hard. Mantle had a lot of regrets to deal with in the last months of his life as he fell ill from years of drinking, but this is not the end of his story.

When Mantle entered the hospital in Dallas in the summer of 1995, he needed and received a new liver to replace his liver, destroyed by alcoholism and cancer.

After just weeks, the doctors discovered that the cancer was still there, and in fact was one of the fastest-spreading kinds of malignancy they had ever seen. "The Mick" was in the bottom of the ninth inning of his life.

Knowing he was dying, Mantle called his old New York Yankee teammate Bobby Richardson, one of the most committed and godly Christians ever to play professional sports. Bobby had shared Christ with Mickey many times over the years, but to no avail. This time it would be different.

Bobby later told me that on a Thursday night in early August, he and his wife, Betsy, visited Mickey at Baylor Hospital at the request of the Mantle family. Mickey was sitting in a chair, very weak.

Betsy knelt beside Mickey's chair and asked him the most important question any person could ever be asked, a question that you and I and everyone on earth will have to answer someday.

"Mickey," she asked, "if you were to die tonight and stand before God, and He were to ask you, 'Why should I let you into My heaven?' what would you say?"

Bobby said that Mickey thought for a moment, and then a smile edged across his face as he began quoting the wonderful promise of John 3:16. Less than three days later, Mickey Mantle was in the presence of the Lord.

When it comes to the issues of eternity, it's vitally important to ask the right questions. It's even more important to get the right answers. Mickey Mantle knew where to turn when it was time to face the issue of eternal life. So did Nicodemus.

It is impossible to study the great night scenes of the Bible without considering the story of Nicodemus in John 3. Here was "a ruler of the Jews" (John 3:1), an honored rabbi in Israel, but a man who was uninformed about basic spiritual reality.

Nicodemus's mind and heart were as dark as the night sky under which he came to Jesus Christ. The apostle John records: "This man came to Jesus by night and said to Him, 'Rabbi, we know that You are a teacher come from God; for no one can do these signs that You do unless God is with him'" (John 3:2).

Now even though this conversation took place almost two thousand years ago, the question Nicodemus asked in verse 4 is as up-to-date as tonight's cable TV offerings: "How can a man be born when he is old? Can he enter a second time into his mother's womb and be born?"

There are a lot of people today who want to know how to be reborn. And if you surf the cable channels long enough, you are sure to find some phony expert telling people how to experience rebirth or reincarnation—or telling them that they are already reborn because they lived a previous existence!

Of course, such nonsense is straight from the enemy of our souls, who wants to confuse and blind the human heart. The reason so many people are looking for a new start is that they are merely existing, just drawing their breath and their salary. But it's not enough just to go to work and come home and then do it all over again the next day. There's more to life than that, and John 3 is the answer.

Nicodemus went to the only reliable, infallible source of information on new birth, the Lord Jesus Christ Himself. I want to look at what Jesus taught Nicodemus in this remarkable night scene from John's Gospel, because what He said has both immediate and eternal implications for your life.

The Reality of the New Birth

Nicodemus was a man who knew religion. He was a Pharisee, meaning that he learned and observed all the particular laws of the Jewish faith. He was a religionist, a legalist, even a hyper-legalist when it came to religious duty.

The Futility of Religion

In Nicodemus we see the futility of religion without the reality of the new birth. As an older man, Nicodemus realized something was still missing in his life. So he came to Jesus by night.

Now people often assume that Nicodemus came to the Lord at night because he was afraid to come by day for fear of what his fellow Pharisees would say. But I don't think so. I believe Nicodemus had some questions on his mind that couldn't wait until the next morning. There was an urgency in the heart of this man to get some answers to the eternal questions of life.

Besides, it was the custom in the Middle East for men to sit around after dinner and discuss issues of life and spirituality. Often rabbis and religious teachers and others would gather and speak of these things. They still do to this day, in fact.

So at night, in the cool of the evening, when the day had settled down, Nicodemus came with his urgent questions to the Lord Jesus Christ. That's the point I want you to see.

Notice that Nicodemus recognized Jesus as "a teacher come from God" (John 3:2). Jesus is far more than that, but for Nicodemus this was a high compliment. We know that Jesus Christ was not a teacher who came from God. He was God who came to teach! He was the God-man, as Nicodemus was about to discover.

No sooner had Nicodemus gotten the words out of his mouth than Jesus took him straight to the reality and necessity of the new birth: "Most assuredly, I say to you, unless one is born again, he cannot see the kingdom of God" (John 3:3).

Jesus was telling Nicodemus that it's not religion or knowing the Scripture that counts, but a new birth; a definite, dynamic decision in which a person passes from spiritual death to spiritual life.

The problem with many people today is that they're enduring religion instead of enjoying a relationship with Jesus Christ through the new birth. Nicodemus was enduring religion, yet he knew something was missing. The Scripture says some people have a form of godliness, but deny its power (2 Tim. 3:5).

You can grow up in church, keep all the rules and regulations and rituals of your particular religion, and still not be born again. Evangelist Billy Graham estimates that up to 80 percent of people who are members of churches in America today have never had a new birth experience in Jesus Christ. They are still in spiritual darkness.

The Necessity of New Birth

Why did Jesus use the term "born again"? Because salvation is much like physical birth. Jesus said we must first be born "of water" (John 3:5). A first-year biology student knows that there is water at birth. So I believe that when Jesus refers to water here, He's referring to physical birth. "Born of water" in verse 5 is parallel to "born of the flesh" in verse 6.

Jesus' point is that a person born physically must also be born spiritually. He said in verse 6, "That which is born of the flesh is flesh [physical birth], and that which is born of the Spirit is spirit [spiritual birth]." Obviously, a person can be born without ever being born again.

So why did Jesus liken salvation to birth? Because when you receive the Lord Jesus Christ as your Savior, something so wonderful, so radical, so revolutionary, and so powerful happens to you that it's like being born all over again. You have a brand-new life. The very presence of God lives within you.

This means the new birth is far more than a religious experience. It is not just changing a few of your old habits. It is not behavior modification or some psychological happening.

The new birth is regeneration—being born a second time, becoming brand new in Jesus Christ, sharing the very life of God. It is a real moment in which people experience a real Savior and a real salvation that lasts forever.

Nicodemus not only came to Jesus because of the failure of his religion to satisfy him. He was also confused about the nature of real faith. He didn't understand the distinction between the physical and the spiritual. When Jesus spoke to him about the new birth, Nicodemus asked, "How can an old man like me be born again?"

You may be asking yourself that same question as you read this book. You may be wondering, "How can I start over again? There's too much water under the bridge, too much sin in my life, too many mistakes and failures and frustrations."

The Glory of the New Birth

That is the glory of the new birth. It can happen to you today. And when you are born again, you know it! Somebody has said, "If you could be born again and not know it, then you could lose your salvation and never miss it." When the new birth happens to you, you know it's happened to you.

One day, humorist Will Rogers was trying to get a passport. He was told he needed a birth certificate. "What fer? Why do I need a birth certificate?"

The man said, "For proof of your birth."

Rogers said, "Well, I'm here, ain't I? Ought to be proof enough."

I know I've been born again because I was there when it happened! Jesus Christ changed my life. Although I was a small child when I came to Christ, it was very real to me. But no matter what your age or your experiences, no one is too sinful or too stubborn but that the new birth can happen to him or her.

The Futility of Other Paths

In the days of Jesus, much like today, people were seeking different ways to find the meaning in life. The Romans, for example, were enamored of their civilization and their system of law and government.

There are many today who think that the rule of law and government will provide the answers to our problems. But we know that government can never meet the deepest needs of a person's heart. Government may take a man out of the ghetto, but it cannot take the ghetto out of a man's heart.

The Greeks of Jesus' day were extremely interested in wisdom and philosophy and education. They believed that learning, a dedication to the pursuit of knowledge, was the path to meaning and purpose in life.

There are many today who believe that the way to solve all the problems we're facing as a society is by education. They believe that if we can just give people a quality education, they will be lifted above their circumstances and be motivated to seek the good and the true and the beautiful.

But education alone ignores mankind's sinful nature. If those who believe in education were right, the best educated people among us would also be the most virtuous. That's hardly the case.

Actually, if you educate people apart from a personal relationship with Jesus Christ, all you're doing is making clever devils out of them. They simply become more sophisticated in committing evil. An education is not salvation.

Then we come to the Jews of that day, like Nicodemus. As we've already seen, they were the religionists. Even today you hear people say, "What America needs is religion."

America does *not* need religion. America needs to be delivered from religion and introduced to the Lord Jesus Christ. Religion is not the answer, just as law and government and wisdom and education are not the answer. Religion without Jesus Christ is meaningless and worthless.

Jesus knew that the answer to meaning and purpose in life lay not in external things, but in the heart, the inner person. That's where He focused Nicodemus's attention when He told him, "You must be born again (John 3:7)." That's the reality of the new birth.

The Simplicity of the New Birth

Think with me also about the simplicity of the new birth. It's such a simple concept that a child can understand it. And yet, it's so profound that it has kept generations of theologians busy trying to explain the miracle of salvation.

Two Parents

The new birth is simple to grasp in the basics. That is, just as we have two parents in physical birth, so there are two parents in spiritual birth: the Word and the Spirit of God.

The Bible describes itself as a seed that brings forth new life. And so, just as the "seed" of the father must be implanted before there can be physical birth, so the seed of God's Word must be implanted in the human heart by the Holy Spirit before a person can be born again.

No one can be saved apart from the Word of God, for "faith comes by hearing, and hearing by the word of God" (Rom. 10:17). This helps explain why so many people can sit in church week after week for years and never experience the new birth.

If you will talk to people who did not come to Christ until they were adults, you will discover that many of them grew up in church, yet never once heard the gospel. Now I'm not trying to point a finger at any particular church, but it's a horrible thing to be in church year after year and never hear the message of salvation because the Word of God is not preached and taught.

You can't preach the Word of God without getting to the gospel. You can't share the message of Scripture without coming face-to-face with the clear need for people to be born again. Jesus spoke so clearly on the necessity of the new birth here in John 3 (see verses 3 and 5 again) that it's impossible to misunderstand Him.

The great nineteenth-century preacher of London, Charles Spurgeon, said, "I take my text anywhere and make a bee-line to the cross." Wherever I am preaching in the Bible, my ultimate goal is to bring people to a new birth experience in Jesus Christ and then to help them grow in that new life.

So the first parent in the new birth is the Word of God. A person must hear and believe the Word. But the other parent in the new birth must be active, because it is possible for a person to hear the Word and not be born again. Until the Holy Spirit begins to move in a human heart, nothing will happen.

It is important for you to understand that you don't come to Christ any time you choose. Jesus said, "No one can come to Me unless the Father who sent Me draws him" (John 6:44). The divine Agent by whom the Father draws people to Christ is the Holy Spirit.

The fact is that no one seeks God apart from the work of God through the Holy Spirit (John 6:44). The Spirit is a necessary parent in the new birth. He works in a person's life, bringing about circumstances that open the heart to Christ, or causing the heart to respond to the Word.

Someone may hear the gospel many times over. But somehow, in that one moment of destiny, that same message takes hold of the person's life by the power of the Holy Spirit, and the miracle of the new birth occurs.

When I was a pastor in Hobart, Oklahoma, one of our church members had a particularly hard time in childbirth. At one point, it looked like the baby wasn't going to make it, but the delivery was finally successful.

This woman was attended by Dr. Van Howard, who had delivered a lot of babies in that area. Van was a friend of mine with whom I often visited. As we talked about this birth and the problems that made it so tough, I said to Van, "You know, this birth was a miracle."

Van looked at me and said, "Pastor, every birth is a miracle." I stood corrected.

Indeed, every physical birth is a miracle of God, and so is every spiritual birth. I still believe in miracles. I know they happen because the greatest miracle is the miracle of salvation, when God brings a new spiritual life into being.

Nothing Complicated

I contend that this process we call the new birth is very simple to grasp and to act upon. We are born again by the Word and the Spirit of God. One of the distinctive marks of a cult or any false religion is the complicated and intricate "salvation" schemes they concoct.

The way many cults keep their members working hard and going around the world is by keeping them in perpetual tension as to whether they've made it or not, whether they have finally achieved "salvation" or whatever they call it.

False religions are generally works-oriented, so they have a system that's ready-made to keep people going. See, if you are trying to gain salvation by good works, how do you know when you've done enough? How do you know when you've piled up enough credits in heaven?

You can't ever know for sure, so you have to keep going. That's the difference between religion and new birth. The former is often very complicated and confusing. You're trying to hit a moving target.

The gospel is so clear and simple. You're either born again or you're not. Salvation is Christ plus nothing or no one else! It is Christ and Christ alone. He died for you, He rose again and lives forever, and by faith you can receive Him as your Savior and Lord. This is the simplicity of the new birth.

The Dignity of the New Birth

When Jesus told Nicodemus that he must be born again, He used a phrase that means literally, "born from above." If you are a child of God through the new birth, you are a member of *the* royal family! Your Father is the King of all creation.

People seem to be endlessly fascinated by the deeds—and misdeeds—of royalty. We want to see kings and queens and princes and princesses up close, to bask in their fame and dignity (although royal dignity has been taking a terrific beating these last few years).

If you are saved, you are royalty in Jesus Christ. The blood of God is coursing through your veins. Your Father owns it all.

"Behold what manner of love the Father has bestowed on us, that we should be called children of God!" writes the apostle (1 John 3:1). "As many as received Him, to them He gave the right to become children of God" (John 1:12). There is dignity in the new birth because when we're saved, we have a new nature. We share the nature of our God.

When you are born, you share the nature of your parents. That's why kids often look and act so much like their parents. If you have experienced the new birth and are a child of God, you're going to begin living and looking like your Father.

I'm not talking about trying to be perfect. God is not interested in the perfection of your life, but He is interested in the direction of your life. If you've been saved, the direction of your life has changed.

What I mean is this: Before you and I were saved, we leaped into sin and loved it. But now that we know Christ, we lapse into sin and loathe it. That's the difference, because Christ has changed the direction of our lives.

Now don't confuse dignity with pride. There is dignity to the new birth, because we are children of the King. But there is nothing for us to be proud about.

Imagine Nicodemus sitting there that night talking to Jesus. As a member of the Sanhedrin, the Jewish council, Nicodemus was doubtless a very dignified man in his long Pharisaic robes. But many of the Pharisees were too proud to admit that a carpenter from a backwater town like Nazareth had anything to say to them.

The dignity I'm talking about is the change you see in a person's life when he or she begins to reflect the beauty and holiness of Christ. There is dignity in the new birth.

The Security of the New Birth

I want to talk about the security of the new birth because it's such an important teaching of Scripture and such a wonderful affirmation of who we are in Christ. By security I simply mean that when we are born into the family of God, we can never be unborn out of the family of God.

Never Unborn

You could no more cease to be the child of your father and mother than you could cease to exist as a person. Now you may be a disobedient child; you may not live with your parents anymore; you may not even know who your real parents are. But you are their child, and you always will be.

The same is true if you are a child of God. Jesus didn't talk about the security of salvation with Nicodemus because that wasn't the question at hand that night. But the concept of security is built into the very imagery Jesus used. You can never be unborn once you are born.

I know many Christians believe you can lose your salvation. But Jesus did not say we must be born again and again and again. We are born once by the power of God, and what God starts, He finishes. "He who has begun a good work in you will complete it until the day of Jesus Christ" (Phil. 1:6).

Never Give Up

We are secure in Christ. God is conforming us to the image of Christ, and He will never give up on us. Sometimes it gets a little tough when He's knocking off all those rough edges, but we are saved and secure. We are in the forever family of God. Don't let anyone cause you to doubt that.

I would hate to think that my salvation depended upon my keeping it. But we are being "kept by the power of God" (1 Peter 1:5). We are being held securely in the Father's hands (John 10:28–29).

Those who believe that a Christian can lose his salvation are actually teaching that salvation is faith plus works, a view with which we have already dealt. They believe we are saved by faith, but if my salvation depends upon what I do and how faithful I am, then my salvation is ultimately dependent upon my works.

The security of the new birth means that whatever is necessary in my life to make me like Christ and get me to heaven, God will bring it to pass. Read Romans 8:30 and you'll see that those whom God justified are the same ones He glorified. The new birth is God's work through and through, and we are secure in Him.

The Urgency of the New Birth

Notice the urgency with which Jesus spoke to Nicodemus. "You *must* be born again" (John 3:7, my emphasis). This is not a suggestion. This is the Word of the Lord Jesus Christ.

No Time to Lose

Why such urgency? Because without the new birth, you will never see the kingdom of God. Without the new birth, there is nothing ahead for you but death and judgment. And you have no guarantee of tomorrow. That means you have no time to lose in coming to Jesus.

If you have been born only once, you'll die twice. You'll die physically, and then you'll die spiritually in what the Bible calls "the second death" (Rev. 20:14). This is eternal death apart from Christ in hell. This is death that lasts forever. Now you know why Jesus spoke with urgency, why He insisted that Nicodemus had to be born again.

If you have been born twice—that is, physically and spiritually—you're going to die just once. You'll die physically if Jesus Christ does not come back in our generation. But you will never die spiritually. You will be alive in the presence of God forever and ever because you've been born again.

Someone once asked the famed preacher John Wesley, "Why are you always preaching on the new birth? Why are you always saying in your sermons, 'You must be born again'?"

Wesley answered with a twinkle in his eye, "Because 'You must be born again.'" That was a wise answer, because that's exactly what Jesus said. He insisted on it, and He insisted on it with urgency. Jesus wanted Nicodemus to be born again that very night.

No Other Way

See, evangelical Christians didn't dream up this idea of being born again. It didn't come from fundamentalists. Some people say, "I'm a Christian, but I'm not one of those 'born-again' kind of Christians."

My friend, there is no other kind of Christian than a born-again Christian! The term "born-again Christian" is actually a redundancy. You're either born again, or you're not a Christian. I didn't say that. Jesus insisted on it. If you're a Christian, you've been born from above by the power of God.

There's an urgency about the new birth because there's no other way to enter heaven. You don't work your way into being born. You can't grow into the new birth. Just like the exact moment of physical birth, spiritual birth is an instantaneous event in which your sins are forgiven, you receive the life of God, and you are changed from the inside out.

Don't think that you can wait to get your life straightened out before you come to Christ. You will never be more ready than you are right now. Everything necessary for your new birth has already been done. You come just as you are.

That is also true even if you're religious. Nicodemus was a good person. He was more religious than most people you will ever meet. But he sat there in the darkness with Jesus that night, trying to process the fact that all of his goodness was not good enough for God. He still needed to be born again.

If it's dark in your soul, if you are sitting in the darkness wondering what is missing, you need to hear Jesus Christ saying to you, "You must be born again." If you will come to Him, all of your darkness will be dispelled and you will begin a new life.

CHAPTER 7

The Christ of Every Crisis:
THE STORM AT SEA

In August 1992, southern Florida was rocked with the most severe storm in recorded American history. Hurricane Andrew ravaged south Florida, damaging or destroying seventy-three thousand homes and inflicting sixteen billion dollars in damage, to say nothing of the many lives lost.

Most of us cannot identify with that kind of devastation, for which we can be thankful. But there was one effect of Hurricane Andrew that we have all experienced. The storm left 1.6 million people in darkness, their electricity knocked out. I am confident that you know what it's like to sit in a dark house during a frightening storm and wonder if daylight will ever come.

I am also confident that you either have experienced, are now experiencing, or will soon experience a different kind of storm—whether it be a domestic storm, a financial storm, a personal storm, or a spiritual storm. The fact is that the storms of life come against all of us, leaving us sitting in the darkness wondering if we will ever see the light again.

I hope you know that faith in Christ is not immunity to the storms of life. God sends storms into our lives, not to destroy us but to correct, develop, and deepen us, as we'll learn in this chapter. Christ promised to see us through the storms, not to keep us out of them.

If you doubt that, look at Matthew 14:22–31, one of the most familiar stories in the New Testament. It begins:

> *Immediately Jesus made His disciples get into the boat and go before Him to the other side, while He sent the multitudes away. And when He had sent the multitudes away, He went up on a mountain by Himself to pray. Now when evening came, He was alone there.*

(Matt. 14:22–23)

We have already seen Jonah delivered from the belly of a great fish and Daniel delivered from a den of lions. So the fact that Jesus Christ, the Lord of glory, could walk on water (Matt. 14:25) should not be a stretch for our faith.

The One who created the waters is certainly able to walk on the water. Jesus performed this miracle—and I wish I could have been there to see it.

The Message of the Miracle

But there's a message to the miracle of Matthew 14. Jesus never performed miracles simply to show off His supernatural power. He only did a miracle when He had a spiritual lesson to teach. There is a parable of teaching in every miracle Jesus performed, just as there is a miracle of teaching in every parable.

So what message did Jesus want to get across to His disciples—and us—in this amazing night scene from the pages of Scripture? To understand the message, I want you to see the disciples sitting in the darkness on the Sea of Galilee.

"The boat was now in the middle of the sea, tossed by the waves, for the wind was contrary" (Matt. 14:24).

These are the circumstances surrounding the message of the miracle in Matthew 14. And the message is that Jesus Christ is the Lord of all the storms of our lives. When we hit the storm, when we are tried, troubled, and tossed like the disciples, when we are confused and scared in the darkness, the Lord Jesus Christ comes to us with a message of hope and assurance and confidence.

I see in this wonderful passage of Scripture four certainties that we can cling to in the midst of the darkness.

God's Aim in the Storm

Certainty number one that we can cling to when our boat is rocking in the darkness is that God has an aim for every storm. Notice that Jesus "made His disciples get into the boat" (Matt. 14:22). This whole trip was Jesus' idea. He had an aim in mind, which was to teach them a lesson on faith and then minister to hurting people when they landed on the other side of the sea (Matt. 14:34–36).

Jesus sent His disciples into the teeth of a storm that He knew full well was on the way. That fact flies in the teeth of the teaching so popular today that God never sends storms our way, that He always wants us happy, healthy, and prosperous.

The truth is that there are times when God may either allow us to enter the darkness of a severe storm, or send the storm Himself. As I study Scripture, I find two kinds of storms that God may send into our lives.

Storms of Correction

The first kind of storm is what I call the storm of correction. Jonah is the most obvious example of a believer encountering God's storm of correction (see Chapter 5). When Jonah rebelled against God and refused to do His will, God hurled that great storm against Jonah and corrected first his thinking, and then his path.

If we are bound and determined to rebel against God and disobey Him, we had better get out our hip-waders and umbrellas! Chances are that God is going to send a storm of correction our way. It may be almost anything, from financial trouble to health problems. In this kind of storm, God's goal is to correct.

Storms of Perfection

At other times we get hit with one of life's storms and we ask, "What did I do wrong?" We wonder and worry about some sin in our lives, when it may not be that at all. It may be instead a storm of perfection.

These storms are sent to perfect and mature us, to make us more like the Lord Jesus Himself. A storm of perfection comes not because we deserve it in the sense of undergoing discipline, but because we need it. Jesus' disciples needed the storm they encountered. It was God's plan to build their faith. But notice what it took to accomplish that aim.

The first thing it took was darkness—the problem of *security*. The disciples were in the "fourth watch" (Matt. 14:25), the darkest time of the night. It was so dark, no doubt, on the Sea of Galilee that they could barely see their hands in front of their faces.

We're told that the disciples were being tormented by the winds. They were being tossed and blown about by the howling storm, and their boat was about to capsize and throw them into the sea. Death seemed to be imminent.

Then there was the problem of *separation*. The disciples were in the middle of the sea, but Jesus was back on the land. The Scripture tells us that Jesus was on the mountain praying, having sent the multitudes and the disciples away (Matt. 14:23). So as far as the Twelve were concerned, He was nowhere to be seen, nowhere to be found.

On an earlier occasion, when the disciples were in the middle of a fierce storm, Jesus was asleep in the boat. So all they had to do was wake Him up and watch Him still the storm (Matt. 8:23–27). But this time they didn't know where Jesus was. They were far from the shore and far from the Savior.

Finally, there was the problem of *silence*. Here they were in the middle of the darkness, in the middle of a stormy sea, crying out in fear, a long way from the shore, and Jesus did not come immediately. He seemed to be taking His time coming to their aid.

Does all of this sound familiar to you? Have you ever been in a storm that made everything around you seem so dark? There seemed to be no answer, no way out. You felt discouraged, depressed, despondent—maybe even faintly disillusioned. There was despair all around you, the dangerous winds were howling, and it seemed that Jesus was nowhere to be found.

We have all experienced times like this. They are never easy, but I want you to see that even in the worst of storms, you can be safe and secure. The disciples were safe and secure on the stormy Sea of Galilee as long as they did one thing. What was it? Let's talk about it.

Obeying in the Storm

The one thing the disciples of Jesus needed to do to be safe was stay in the boat. Why? Because that's what Jesus told them to do. He said, "Get in the boat and go to the other side." To obey Jesus was to stay in that boat.

The Scripture says, "He who does the will of God abides forever" (1 John 2:17). What if those disciples had tried to turn the boat around and go back? They would have been in deep trouble. What if they had tried to jump out of the boat and swim for shore? Jesus would have been looking for twelve new followers, because they would have perished.

What the disciples needed to discover in the midst of their storm was that God had a plan in all of it. But God's plan included staying in the boat, not bailing out.

You and I will never know the plan of God for our lives. We will never experience the purpose and the power of God in our lives, until we get to the place where we are absolutely stranded and utterly dependent on Him.

Have you ever been there? When you are stranded on the power and goodness of God, you pray, "God, if You don't come through, my boat is sunk. But no matter what, I'm going to stay in the boat. I'm going to believe You and trust You."

When you come to that point, you will find out something about God that you can't learn any other way. When you come to the place that He is all you have, you will discover that He is all you need.

I don't know anyone who enjoys riding out a raging storm. But as the song says, if we never had a problem we would never know that God could solve them.

Praying for You

You say, "That sounds good, Jack. But how can I be so sure of God's care and God's help when I can't see Him in the darkness?" Because Jesus is praying for you.

Go back to Matthew 14:23 and you'll recall that while the action was breaking loose on the sea, Jesus was up on a mountain praying for His disciples. He was absent from them in person, but He was with them in power because He was praying for them.

Guess what Jesus is doing while your boat is reeling in the darkness? He's praying for you! Even though you may not be able to sense His presence, Jesus is with you.

I know that because Hebrews 7:25 tells us Jesus "lives to make intercession for [us]." He's at the right hand of the Father, interceding for you. If you knew that Jesus was in the next room right now, calling out your name to the Father in prayer, wouldn't you be confident that there was no storm, no challenge too great but that you could stand against it?

Distance makes no difference to Jesus. He is praying for you the way He prayed for Peter, that your faith would not fail in the hour of trial (Luke 22:32). Jesus is asking the Father to keep you by His power (John 17:11).

So regardless of the storm you're battling today, you can have the certainty that God has a plan in it for you.

God's Adequacy Through the Storm

The second certainty you can have in your storm is that God is present in the midst of it. When it seemed like hope was lost, Jesus came out to the disciples, walking on the water (Matt. 14:25).

The Right Time

Jesus came because His purpose in delaying had been fulfilled. He came at exactly the right moment.

Sometimes Jesus delays so that God's greater glory can be realized, as in the case of Lazarus (John 11:4–6). While Lazarus was sick, Jesus purposely delayed going to Bethany in order that He might raise Lazarus from the dead and glorify God.

The Bible says that Jesus Himself was born in Bethlehem "when the fullness of the time had come" (Gal. 4:4). The Jews had prayed and looked for the Messiah for centuries. But at the precise moment that fulfilled His purposes, God sent His Son. Time means nothing to God. But timing is everything with God.

Several years ago, there was a movie about an alien who comes to the United States from outer space. As a part of the story of how this alien adapts to life on earth, we see him learning how to drive. He's got an American in the car with him, and he's driving like a madman, running through yellow and even red traffic lights. When the American asks this alien why he is driving like this, the alien tells him, "Well, I've been watching you Americans and I understand your traffic light system. Red means stop, green means go, and yellow means drive faster."

We're in a hurry, aren't we? Any time there's a caution light, we want to drive faster. But sometimes God puts a signal light in front of us to cause us to slow down or even stop. The psalmist said, "He makes me to lie down" (Ps. 23:2). God may send a storm to make us stop and think and pray and realize His presence.

The Right Message

God puts a premium on patience, to teach us to wait on Him in those troubled times. But notice that not only does

He come to us at just the right time, He always comes with just the right message.

Jesus said to the disciples in verse 27 of Matthew 14, "Be of good cheer!" It was a message of cheer. Now Jesus was not just saying, "Come on, guys. I know you don't feel it, but put a smile on your face." He was speaking of that inner happiness, that inner joy we can have in spite of circumstances.

Jesus didn't give His men a speech or a theological discourse on the problem of suffering in the world. He didn't rag on them for being afraid. In the middle of their storm, He said, "Cheer up! I'm here." And He is saying the same thing to the saints of God today. *He is able*!

Jesus also came with a message of confidence, "It is I," and a message of courage, "Do not be afraid." Now when Jesus said, "It is I," He was literally saying, "I Am."

If you know your Bible, that phrase will be familiar to you. It was a declaration of Jesus' deity. He was identifying Himself as the great "I AM" (Ex. 3:14), *Yahweh*, the precious covenant name of God.

In other words, this One walking on the water to the disciples was not just a miracle worker, but God in the flesh. Wherever Jesus showed up, God was there. Because He is Lord of heaven and earth, He is Lord of all the circumstances of life.

God is present with us. Jesus promised, "I am with you always, even to the end of the age" (Matt. 28:20). When you're hurting, when the darkness is so thick you can't see your own hand let alone anything else, Jesus comes to you at the moment of your need and says, "I AM." *He is able*!

Not only is He able. He is available. "I AM" whatever you need (Phil. 4:19). Jesus is the Christ of today. He's not just the One who died on the cross and rose again in history, or the One who's coming again someday. He's the One who lives in our hearts today. He is the Christ of every crisis. Whatever your storm, you can be certain of God's aim and God's adequacy.

God's Authority over the Storm

In addition, you can be certain of God's authority over your dark storm.

The fact that Jesus went to the disciples walking on the sea teaches us something very important. As my friend Adrian Rogers says, "It teaches us that everything that is over our heads is under His feet."

You can't drown as long as your head is above the water. When you're teaching your children to swim, what do you teach them to do? You teach them to keep their heads above the water and they'll be fine.

In the same way, our Head, the Lord Jesus Christ, is above the water. He said, "I have overcome the world" (John 16:33; notice, by the way, that Jesus prefaces this with the same message: "Be of good cheer"). All of that water, all of that darkness and storm that was over the heads of the disciples, was beneath Jesus.

And today all of the problems, all of the crises, all of the challenges of life, are under His authority. Jesus walked right across the stormy Sea of Galilee. He made a pathway right through the storm. He is our everything for our anything.

God's Accomplishment from the Storm

Finally, we can be certain of God's desire to accomplish His best for us and to do in us what we could not do unless we were "seasoned" by the storm. As I said earlier, Jesus was not just showing off His divine power. He wants to teach us how to walk on the water.

Peter was the one who wanted to give it a try. Up to this time, the disciples were to stay in the boat. But now Jesus gave Peter permission to get out of the boat and come to Him. "Peter answered Him and said, 'Lord, if it is You, command me to come on the water.' So He said, 'Come'" (Matt. 14:28–29).

Getting out of the Boat

You can't walk on the water until you get out of the boat. Jesus is trying to teach us how to get above the circumstances of life, how to put the storms under our feet, how to increase our faith so that we can live victoriously for Him.

Jesus wants us to stop playing it safe all the time, to step out when He bids us come. He wants to show us that nothing is impossible if God is in it. As one great devotional writer said, "We never test the resources of God until we attempt the impossible."

You say, "But Peter sank, didn't he?" Yes, he took his eyes off of Jesus and he sank (Matt. 14:30–31). And he was rebuked for his "little faith."

Do you know something? Peter still walked farther on the water than any of the rest of us have, because he followed the Lord's command. It is better to sink doing the will of God than to shrink back, wondering what might have been if we had only trusted and believed God.

Perhaps God has sent you into a storm to shake you out of your complacency and move you forward in your Christian walk.

Learning to Walk on Water

There are two kinds of Christians: those who watch things happen, and those who make things happen. Those who make things happen are the ones who believe God enough to get out of the boat and walk on water when Jesus calls.

That is faith. In our storms, Jesus is teaching us the faith that is willing to test the resources of God, attempt the impossible for God, and do the supernatural in the power of Jesus Christ.

When I was a pastor in West Palm Beach, Florida, a film company asked us if they could use our buildings to film part of a movie. The star of the movie was Burt Reynolds, who lived there in the Palm Beach area. It was a fascinating thing to watch these people work, and in the course of that movie I met the stuntman who doubled for Burt Reynolds.

Stan Barrett is known as one of the world's greatest stuntmen. He holds the record for breaking the sound barrier on the ground. He actually strapped an engine that looked like a rocket on his back and broke the sound barrier.

This man seemingly had no fear of jumping off buildings, jumping out of airplanes, and so forth. He was to fall off the roof of a building in the film, so one day I asked him, "How do you ever get up the courage to step off that roof?"

I was especially interested to know because earlier they had tried to get me to jump off the roof and land on one of those huge air mattresses. I passed on that one!

When I asked him that question, he said, "You know, the first step is the only step you have to take." Just one step will do it. Then he went on to say something I'll never forget. "I'll jump from any height as long as I have a good catcher beneath me."

That is what we as Christians ought to be able to say. "I will jump from any height as long as I know that the Lord Jesus is there to catch me." Peter calls it "casting all your care upon Him, for He cares for you" (1 Peter 5:7).

This incredible night scene in Matthew 14 actually ends up with the disciples on their faces, worshiping Jesus as the Son of God (v. 33). That's where we need to end up, because one day at the right time, at the exact moment on God's calendar, Jesus is going to come back walking not on the sea, but on the clouds.

One more time He is going to say what He said to Peter in Matthew 14:29: "Come." Then all of us who know the Lord Jesus Christ will rise to meet Him, to be with Him forever. Then the waves will stop and everything will be calm. The last storm will be over.

CHAPTER 8

Failure Is Not Final:
PETER'S SECOND CHANCE

You probably have guessed by now that I am a huge baseball fan. One of the things I love about the game is that because baseball is played almost every day, yesterday's goats can become today's heroes. Failure doesn't usually last long in baseball.

In fact, one of baseball's great hitters once gave a great answer to the question of why he chose baseball as a career. "Where else can you fail seven out of ten times and still be considered a success?" He was referring, of course, to the mathematics involved in being a .300 hitter, the benchmark of greatness for any batter.

Baseball statistics are fascinating to me because they reveal the extent to which a person can taste defeat and still come out a winner. For instance, in his illustrious career, Babe Ruth compiled almost twice as many strikeouts as he did home runs. Ruth whiffed 1,330 times, but no one remembers that because with that same powerful swing he hit 714 home runs.

What about Cy Young, for whom the annual award to the best pitcher in each league is named? Young was a legendary figure who won an astounding total of 511 games, far more than any other pitcher in history.

However, Cy Young also *lost* more games than any other pitcher, an equally astounding total of 313 defeats. And Babe Ruth failed almost twice as often as he succeeded as a home run hitter. But those numbers still put Ruth and Young in the Hall of Fame.

What is true on the baseball diamond is true in the spiritual realm. Failure need never be final in the life of the Christian. We are going to see from God's Word that if you are a child of His, you do not have to be overcome by failure. You don't have to hide in the darkness.

I want you to know that defeat in your life can be turned to victory in Jesus Christ. Even if you run off into the darkness and try to hide, Jesus will come looking for you and bring you back. With Him, failure is not final. You can be a victor over failure instead of its victim, because victory is your spiritual birthright in Christ.

Victory out of Defeat

They say everybody loves a winner. But I'll tell what I think people love more than a winner. They love to see the person who, as the old Timex wristwatch commercials used to say, "Takes a licking and keeps on ticking."

Perhaps the most beautiful example of that truth in all of Scripture is Simon Peter, who failed the Lord miserably, as we will see in John 18.

Peter denied the Lord and proclaimed that he never knew Him. And yet, Peter made the greatest comeback in all of history. He bounced back from his failure to be the powerful preacher of Pentecost and one of the pillars of the first-century church.

So I want to examine first Peter's failure, that we might be warned by it and avoid failing the Lord. Then I want to talk about Peter's recovery from his failure, that we might be encouraged to realize that failure is never final when we walk with the Lord.

The Causes of Failure

What happened to Peter? What would cause this man who was so close to Jesus, who no doubt loved the Savior with all of his heart, to stumble in his faith and commitment and deny the Lord? Let's examine our text concerning Peter's experience on the awful night of Jesus' betrayal and arrest and of Peter's denial.

> *Simon Peter followed Jesus, and so did another disciple. [That other disciple no doubt is the author of this Gospel, John the beloved.] Now that disciple was known to the high priest, and went with Jesus into the courtyard of the high priest.*
>
> (John 18:15)

Peter didn't just fall into his night of denials by accident. Jesus had prepared him for it by telling him earlier that same night, "Simon, Simon! Indeed, Satan has asked for you, that he may sift you as wheat. But I have prayed for you, that your faith should not fail" (Luke 22:31–32a).

Peter's Self-Sufficiency

So Peter was warned. But one of Peter's perpetual problems was that he trusted himself too much. He was self-sufficient. He thought his spiritual power was self-contained. In this case, he overdosed on self-confidence.

We know that because of another incident that happened on this same night, during the Last Supper. Jesus and His disciples were reclining around the table in the Upper Room when Jesus said, "All of you will be made to stumble because of Me this night" (Matt. 26:31a).

Peter reacted immediately. "Even if all are made to stumble because of You, I will never be made to stumble" (Matt. 26:33). Peter was saying, "Lord, I can see where these other guys might cave in. But not me. I would be the last guy on earth to turn You in. Why, I'll die with You if I have to!" (Matt. 26:35).

I think Peter really believed that. He was utterly confident that he would never betray the Lord. But he didn't know the treachery of his own heart. The Bible says, "The heart is deceitful above all things, and desperately wicked; who can know it?" (Jer. 17:9).

Peter loved Jesus, but he was not prepared for the darkness of the night he would face. And he was not aware of the darkness of his heart. Self-sufficiency set him up for his failure.

This is a danger we all face. The Scripture says, "Let him who thinks he stands take heed lest he fall" (1 Cor. 10:12).

There is a potential for evil in every one of us. Let any of us take his eyes off the Lord Jesus Christ, begin to neglect the spiritual disciplines, and trust in his own strength, and given the right circumstances, failure, always lurking in the shadows, will leap out and overtake him. That is what pride will do to the Christian.

Peter said that he would never deny Christ. He boasted in his faith, but his faith failed. When we are most aware of our spiritual weakness, that's when we're the strongest. Jesus said, "Blessed are the poor in spirit" (Matt. 5:3a). Happy are those who understand their spiritual poverty.

It is when we think we are the strongest, when we think we've got it all together and we drop our guard spiritually, that failure knocks us off our feet. Then we are humbled.

Peter's failure came to bring him to his knees and prepare him for his future. His failure deflated his self-sufficiency.

Peter's Self-Reliance

Jesus took Peter, James, and John with Him to the Garden of Gethsemane that night and said, "Stay here and watch with Me" (Matt. 26:38b). Then He went a little farther into the garden and prayed with agonizing tears and sweat oozing through the pores of His skin.

While Jesus agonized, expecting these disciples to pray, Peter and the other two fell asleep. Peter was so close to Christ in the moment of His anguish he could hear His sobs and see His tears glistening in the moonlight. Yet because of his self-reliance, Peter was prayerless.

Jesus taught us to pray, "Do not lead us into temptation, but deliver us from the evil one" (Matt. 6:13a). Every day we face incredible temptations and illusions from Satan.

To be victorious over these temptations we must be on our faces before God. We are no match for Satan on our own. To rely upon our spiritual power is insanity in the face of the "roaring lion" who roams about seeking to devour us (1 Peter 5:8).

You and I are no stronger than our prayer life. When we begin to neglect prayer and the discipline of our devotional life with God, that is when self-reliance sets in.

Why don't we pray the way God has commanded us to pray? Because we figure we've got it all together. Everything seems to be in place. Things are going our way. In our self-reliance we begin to depend upon ourselves and just embark upon a new day or new week, never dedicating and delivering it to Christ.

When this happens, we are set up to fall because we stop praying. It happened to Simon Peter, and it can happen to you and me.

Prayer, on the other hand, produces power. We are enabled and energized by the power of God in prayer as we express our trust in Him and surrender our will to His will. We are made strong to face any temptation or test that comes.

Peter's Self-Confidence

Another reason Peter failed was what I'm going to call self-confidence.

When Jesus was arrested, the disciples fled. The fear was too much for them. The crowd began to gather for the trial, and Peter decided to follow. He was confident he could hang around outside the courtyard of Annas (see John 18:13) while Jesus was inside facing His torturers, and yet not be found out.

According to John 18:16–17, "The other disciple [John himself], who was known to the high priest, went out and spoke to her who kept the door, and brought Peter in. Then the servant girl who kept the door said to Peter, 'You are not also one of this Man's disciples, are you?' He said, 'I am not.'"

Now Peter could have stepped inside the courtyard without denying Jesus at the door. John had gone in without denying Him. And Peter could have stood there without moving over to warm his hands with the soldiers and the enemies of Christ (John 18:18, 25). John apparently did not do that.

Peter was the one in need of the spiritual lesson, not John. First we see him just walking with the crowd on the periphery. Then we see him standing with the crowd. And finally, we see Peter cozying up with the crowd as he flung himself into the very face of temptation.

So while Jesus was being tried by men, Simon Peter was being tried and tempted by the devil. He was following the downward path of the ungodly man, described so poignantly in Psalm 1.

The Crowd of Failure

Do you see the downward progression in Peter's life on that awful night? As he identified more and more with sinful men and those who scorned the Lord Jesus, he moved farther from Jesus until ultimately, he had denied his Lord three times.

My point is that Peter's denial was a process. Most of us don't just suddenly blow our testimony. Generally speaking, we don't fall into sin or spiritual collapse all at once. Most people fail because they've got a slow leak, or there is a character flaw that has not been dealt with and it surfaces when the circumstances are right.

People have spiritual earthquakes because they have secret "faults." Peter had a secret fault, which as we have seen was a bad case of "self-itis." He was also hanging out with the wrong people at the wrong place and the wrong time.

The Bible says we are to "abstain from all appearance of evil" (1 Thess. 5:22 KJV). That is, every time it even looks like evil is about to raise its ugly head, we're to get out of there.

That also means we are to run when evildoers make their appearance. Don't get caught warming yourself at the fire of the compromisers and those who would deny the Lord, or you might get burned.

Certainly we are to be friends with those who don't know Christ in order to bring them to Him. Psalm 1 doesn't tell us to shun all contact with the ungodly. The issue is who is influencing whom? When it comes to the crowd, we are to be the influencer, not the one influenced.

I hope you choose your friends wisely. Proverbs 13:20 warns us, "The companion of fools shall be destroyed." The road to failure is well traveled and well populated. The person who runs with the wrong crowd is on the verge of spiritual collapse.

You show me the kind of kids that Christian kids hang out with, and I'll show you the kind of people they will soon become if they're not already there.

This admonition is not just for the young. Whether you're a teenager or a business executive, if you are hanging out with the wrong people I promise you that you will soon be like them.

That is why it is so important that you have Christian friends and involve yourself in the church. Don't neglect your fellow believers in the body of Christ, your sisters and brothers in the family of God, the ones who love you the most.

Simon Peter ended up denying his faith, denying his Lord, and wrecking his witness because he was in the wrong place at the wrong time with the wrong people. That's simple enough to grasp, but not always simple to implement.

The Cost of Failure

Peter's downhill slide continued once he warmed his hands next to those of Christ's enemies. We have already seen his first denial in John 18:17. But he plunged on recklessly, at great cost.

Bitter Regret

John records in verses 25 and 27 that Peter denied the Lord a second time and then a third time. And no sooner had Peter gotten that last denial out of his mouth (with oaths and profanity, according to Matthew 26:74) than "a rooster crowed" (John 18:27). Everything had happened just as Jesus predicted (John 13:38). No wonder Peter "went out and wept bitterly" (Matt. 26:75).

He was the most miserable man on the face of the earth. His joy was gone. His victory was gone. His testimony was gone.

It has been well said that the most miserable person on earth is not the unsaved man or woman. The most miserable person on earth is the Christian who is out of fellowship with God. That's where Peter landed after his failure.

Loss of Fellowship

You know what I'm talking about because we've all been there. Maybe we didn't deny the Lord with oaths and curses as Peter did, but we have all experienced times when God seemed like a distant relative and we failed to live for Christ.

That loss of fellowship with God is costly. Deep down, we know we're not being faithful witnesses for the Lord Jesus Christ, that if our friends found out we were Christian, they would be surprised. We are doing the same things they do, using the same language they use, displaying the same attitudes they display, and hanging out with the same crowd they hang out with.

A Christian in this condition is a miserable and defeated person. And sadly, unless that failure is addressed, believers in this condition often slip away into the darkness, like Peter, to hide their shame. They just sort of disappear. As a pastor, I've seen it happen time and again.

You don't see these folks at church anymore. And before you know it, they've changed their circle of friends. Then you can barely remember that they belonged to Jesus Christ.

Simon Peter's failure cost him dearly. He was broken up over his great denial. Spiritual failure is always costly, but aren't you thankful Peter's story doesn't end there?

The Cure for Failure

There is one more chapter to Peter's story. His failure was not final. It was curable. God went to work after Peter's denial and restored the apostle by His grace—just as He will do for you and me. The person who has failed and has been forgiven understands the love of the Lord Jesus Christ.

The Love of Christ

I don't think Peter fully understood the love of Jesus until he had failed Him. I believe that the crowing of that rooster, while signaling the completion of Peter's failure, was also a message of reassurance to him as he went out to weep and repent.

How did the rooster's crow reassure Peter? As he began to clear his head and think about what had happened, the crowing reminded Peter that Jesus was in control. He had said this would happen. Perhaps also it brought to mind Jesus' words found in Luke 22:32—He was praying for Peter.

In other words, as Peter put all of this together he was reassured that none of this caught Jesus by surprise, and that it wasn't over for him.

The rooster's crow was also a sign of renewal for Peter, because it signified the dawning of a new day. Peter would yet come out of the darkness into the clear light of the love of Christ and the forgiveness of God.

Peter would discover that even though he denied he even knew the name of Jesus, the Savior never stopped loving him. And in that beautiful *daylight* scene in John 21:15–19, Jesus gave Peter three opportunities to reaffirm his love, while at the same time reassuring Peter that he was forgiven and restored to his ministry.

Let me tell you, we can do nothing to get away from the grace of the Lord Jesus Christ. He loves us, sometimes in spite of ourselves. His love is unconditional.

No matter how you may have sinned and failed, it's never too late to come back to Christ. There is a place of beginning again for you if you will be honest and repentant before Him.

Honesty and Repentance

One of the remarkable things about Peter is that he candidly related this whole shameful episode, including his falling asleep in the Garden of Gethsemane. Let me show you what I mean.

The apostle John was there when it happened, so he could tell it firsthand. Matthew was an apostle too, so I'm sure he heard the story within days. But like Luke, the gospel writer Mark was a later convert to the faith.

Later Mark became Peter's ministry companion. Peter even called him "my son" in 1 Peter 5:13. Mark relied upon Peter for much of the information recorded in the Gospel of Mark.

For instance, it is Mark who records that when Jesus found the three disciples sleeping in the garden, He addressed Peter specifically (Mark 14:37). And along with the other Gospels, Mark records Peter's denial, which Peter must have told him about in detail.

That is honesty. Peter the "Rock" had fractured and crumbled under pressure. But Peter was more than just honest. He was repentant. His bitter tears were tears of deep remorse and repentance. He didn't take the attitude of the '90s "trash talk show" guests who say, "Yeah, I did it. So what?"

Peter's repentance stands in bold contrast to the fate of another disciple who failed Jesus miserably that same week. Judas also denied the Lord by betraying Him to His accusers for a price. Both Peter and Judas failed, but there was a distinct difference between Judas the failure and Peter the failure.

What is that difference? Judas made failure the end of his life. He was so overcome with grief and the tragedy of his treachery that the Bible says he went out and hanged himself (Matt. 27:5).

Jesus said Judas went to his rightful place because he was the "son of perdition" (John 17:12). But I believe that had Judas turned back to Christ in repentance and genuine faith, he could have been saved even though he had betrayed his Lord.

As for Judas, failure was final. He made his failure the end of his life. The other man, Simon Peter, made his failure the beginning of his life.

If you are saved, Jesus will never deny you. You can never "fail" your way out of His hand. He will remain faithful—

and He will be there when you are ready to come back to Him.

A Question for You

Let me pose a question to you. Will your failure be the end or the beginning for you? Will you walk away into the night, away from Christ, or will you allow Him to restore you and find full recovery and victory out of defeat?

You need to answer that question because Satan desires to have you, to rob you of your joy and your testimony, even to destroy you, just as he desired to have Peter.

Jesus is praying for you (John 17:20), even as He prayed for Peter. He ever lives to make intercession for His saints (Heb. 7:25). Even when we fail, He makes all things appropriate in their time (see Eccl. 3:1). The Scripture says He gives us "beauty for ashes" (Isa. 61:3).

Romans 8:28 can be written over the life of every Christian who fails but turns from that failure in repentance and faith. God can make "all things work together for good to those who love [Him]." He can turn even our failure around for His glory and ultimately our good.

Failure does not have to end in disgrace. There is always another chance when you know the Lord. There's always the second half of the game to play, always another at bat, always another opportunity to snatch victory from the jaws of defeat. Peter was knocked down, but he wasn't knocked out. He got back up and became a winner—and so can you!

CHAPTER 9

Praying Through the Darkness:
With Christ in Suffering

It was a crime that shocked and sickened even the most crime-weary residents of the Dallas-Ft. Worth metroplex.

Late in 1995, our area was afflicted with another series of driveway robberies, in which the thief would accost and rob a person or a couple as they pulled into their driveway at night.

Unfortunately for the young couple I want to tell you about, robbery was not the only motive of the three men who accosted them as they pulled into the driveway of their home.

Threatening to kill their victims, the men bound this husband and wife and put them into the trunk of their car. Then for the next two hours, the thieves drove from one ATM machine to another, using the couple's card to steal money from their account.

The woman managed to kick the glass out of the taillight so they could get some air, and she and her husband sang hymns and quoted Scripture to each other as they waited for what they feared would be their deaths.

The wife thought especially of their new baby, who in the providence of God was at home in the care of a grandmother, who was herself completely unaware of what had happened in the driveway.

After getting all the money they could, the men drove this couple to a lonely field, where they brutally and repeatedly raped the wife. She had mentioned her baby to the men as she and her husband pleaded for their lives, and her plea struck home with one of the assailants.

"I have a son myself," he told her, "so we won't kill you." They then abandoned the couple and fled.

The next morning I visited that couple's home, for they are members of our church in Dallas. The community was reacting in horror and outrage at the brutality of crime. I didn't know what to expect as I entered that home. Would I find a beautiful young Christian couple with their faith destroyed?

I did not. Instead, I walked into a home bathed in an incredible sense of serenity and peace. Please don't misunderstand. There were deep physical and emotional bruises. These precious people had been brutalized and traumatized. But they told me, "Pastor, we want God to be glorified more than anything else."

Now you may be thinking, *That's wonderful, but they were probably still in shock. The anger and grief and doubts had not set in yet.* I was also concerned at the time that they were in shock, and that despair might later devour them.

Obviously, the lives of this young couple will in some ways never be the same. But I can tell you that as I write this chapter, more than six months after the ordeal, their faith has not wavered. They made good on their desire to glorify God. Word went out all over the Dallas area of their faith in the midst of unspeakable terror.

Not only that, but this dear young woman is at this moment undergoing the further ordeal of having to repeat her story three times on the witness stand as the three defendants are being tried separately. Our church has provided counseling for this couple and every other form of support we can give them, and I can only watch in amazement as God works in their lives.

When called upon to go through such an experience with a friend or loved one, we are often tempted to put our arms around them and say, "I understand what you're going through." Now even though we may say that, unless we have experienced the same grief, we know in our hearts that it is impossible to really comprehend the depth of that person's sorrow.

It's good to comfort a hurting friend, to be there and put an arm of love around someone who is hurting. But more often than not, we cannot enter fully into their suffering and say we understand it.

That is why we need to approach people who are suffering greatly not as teachers with lessons to give out, but as students who need to listen and learn. Nowhere is that more true than in the Garden of Gethsemane, where our Lord Jesus Christ agonized in prayer as He faced the Cross.

We could never understand the depths of our Savior's agony on that lonely night in the garden if we were to live a thousand years. But though we cannot identify with Jesus' suffering, we can learn from it lessons that will sustain us in our night of suffering, and help us comfort others with the same comfort (2 Cor. 1:3–4).

Entering Gethsemane

That night of our Lord's agony began in the Upper Room, where He and the disciples observed the Last Supper. Following the meal, Jesus and His disciples made their way down from that room and crossed the Kidron Valley in Jerusalem (John 18:1). At that time of the year, the brook of the same name would have been full and rushing with water through the valley.

It was nearing midnight on Thursday night. The Cross was just hours away for Jesus. The cool of the evening surrounded Him and the eleven (Judas having gone to betray Him) as they made their way to the Garden of Gethsemane on the Mount of Olives.

On Holy Ground

There in the garden our Lord found a very private place that perhaps He had come to on other occasions. It was a place of solitude and solace where, on this final night before the Cross, our Lord entered a time of deep prayer.

It was midnight, but far darker than the night was the darkness of soul Jesus faced that evening as He entered into deep prayer and surrender to the Father:

> *Then they came to a place which was named Gethsemane; and He said to His disciples, "Sit here while I pray." And He took Peter, James, and John with Him, and He began to be troubled and deeply distressed.*

(Mark 14:32–33)

As we walk with our Lord into Gethsemane on this night, we are reminded that we are on holy ground. This is a place of sacred prayer; here in the garden we witness the agony and the anguish of our Savior as He prepared Himself for the Cross. This is a night scene unlike any we have studied so far. Indeed, there will never be another night in history like this night.

I once visited a garden on the side of the Mount of Olives—perhaps the very same garden in which our Lord prayed—and saw there the gnarled olive trees. I was reminded as I looked at those olive trees, some of which are believed to be more than two thousand years old, that those trees watched as our Lord poured out His soul before the Father.

Gethsemane means "oil press." The olives from those trees would be put in an olive press, where they would be crushed and pulverized so that the olive oil could be extracted. There in the "olive press" of suffering in Gethsemane, our Lord was broken and crushed so that He might give His life for us. His was a sorrow that none of us will ever know.

It was not the grief of physical anguish that pressured and crushed the Lord. It was the emotional pain, the suffering of His soul. We know that emotional pain can be much more damaging even than physical pain, and the deep distress and grief of the Savior is obvious in this account in Mark 14.

All we can do is take off our shoes, like Moses standing on holy ground at the burning bush, and worship the Lord Jesus Christ. We can only cry out with the hymn writer, "Man of sorrows! What a name, for the Son of God who came, ruined sinners to reclaim! Hallelujah, what a Savior!" (Phillip P. Bliss, "Man of Sorrows, What a Name!").

A Night of Sorrow

The prophet Isaiah, looking ahead to this hour and to the Cross, called Him "a Man of sorrows and acquainted with grief" (Isa. 53:3). Of course we know that in His earthly life Jesus knew joy, although the Bible never records that He laughed.

The Scripture does say of Jesus that God anointed Him "with the oil of gladness more than [His] companions" (Heb. 1:9). And Jesus Himself gave His joy to His disciples (John 15:11). I'm certain that Jesus laughed many times around campfires with His disciples and along the road as they followed Him.

Now, however, He came to His time of sorrow. On this night Jesus became acquainted with grief in a way He had never known before as God laid on Him "the iniquity of us all" (Isa. 53:6).

Seeking Companionship

As Jesus entered the garden, He left His disciples at the gate with the admonition, "Sit here while I pray." He took with Him Peter, James, and John, that trinity of followers who knew Christ so well. Jesus knew that they would pass along what they saw and experienced to the others.

It is significant to me that Jesus took these three human companions with Him into His darkness. Jesus felt the desperate need to commune with His heavenly Father. But in the dark night of His soul, He also desired fellowship with these men.

Though closely communing with the Father, Jesus needed the human touch at that time as well. How blessed it is when we go through the darkness to have friends in the body of Christ who will stand with us!

Jesus wanted more than these disciples' physical presence. He sought their spiritual support. This was a time for intense prayer. As they arrived at the place of prayer, Jesus told them, "My soul is exceedingly sorrowful, even to death. Stay here and watch" (Mark 14:34).

Jesus' disciples needed to pray and prepare themselves not only for this hour, but for the events that would unfold as He faced the Cross. Yet, we know that Peter, James, and John failed to pray in the garden. Surely this contributed to their collapse later on when Christ was arrested and they all fled—save John, who would stand at the foot of the cross.

What a powerful lesson for us as we face our dark hour, our personal Gethsemanes. When the darkness surrounds us and it's difficult to see God, we need to hear our Lord saying to us, "Watch and pray."

There in the garden, Jesus not only prepared Himself by prayer, He taught us how to pray through the darkness, because all of us are called upon to take up our crosses daily and follow Jesus.

The Horror of Gethsemane

As Jesus went farther into the garden, He "began to be troubled and deeply distressed" (Mark 14:33). Jesus had always anticipated this moment. The plan of salvation had been drawn up in eternity past. And from His youth on, Jesus realized that His mission was to suffer and die. Now that moment had come.

The weight and the intensity of the sorrow that lay just ahead began to crush Jesus. Adding to His pain, no doubt, was Judas's desertion. The betrayer had already slipped away into the night to turn Jesus over to the Romans and the Jewish authorities. And Jesus knew the other disciples, men into whom He poured His life, would soon run in fear and hide in shame.

But greater than the betrayal and the desertions was the fact that Jesus knew He would become sin for us (2 Cor. 5:21). The reality of the sin He was bearing caused Jesus to be troubled and distressed. The English words barely convey the depth of Jesus' suffering.

This is unusually strong language in the original. Jesus was appalled at the prospect of bearing sin and being separated from the Father. He was feeling literally "not at home," horrified that He must be abandoned by God the Father, who cannot look on sin.

Jesus lived in perfect fellowship with and obedience to His Father. Now the reality of the separation left Jesus with a crushing sense of isolation and loneliness in Gethsemane.

There are two kinds of loneliness. The first is the loneliness of being physically separated from others, being all alone. But the second kind of loneliness, what psychologists call "cosmic loneliness," is much deeper. It's that sense of being not at home, of being all alone in the universe.

You can be in a crowd or at a party and feel cosmic loneliness. You can be at church, in the midst of a great throng worshiping and singing hymns of praise to God, and still stand there feeling isolated, empty, and alone.

Our Lord experienced that kind of loneliness and isolation in Gethsemane as already, He was becoming estranged from God the Father. Already, the sorrows of the Cross surrounded and engulfed Him as the "cup" of suffering—the cup symbolic of all His suffering gathered into one place—was placed before Him.

Looking into the Cup

What was in that cup that caused our Lord to be so horrified? What did Jesus see when He looked into that cup that repulsed His soul and caused Him to shrink away in agony?

Certainly He saw His death. The Bible says that Jesus tasted death for everyone (Heb. 2:9). He was about to drink the cup of death as no one before has or will ever drink of it.

In that cup Jesus also saw a cosmic spiritual battle. In addition to His growing estrangement and sense of alienation from the Father, Jesus was battling the powers of darkness that were invading His soul.

Satan himself, like a roaring lion, was roaming that quiet garden that evening. He had been unable to turn Jesus away from the Cross in the wilderness temptation. But perhaps, if Jesus could not be swayed by the offer of bread and kingdoms and public acclaim, perhaps now in Jesus' hour of great agony, Satan could turn Him from the Cross.

This had been Satan's goal since the day of Jesus' birth. If he could somehow tempt Jesus to take another road, then all of mankind would perish. So added to His other griefs, Jesus was fighting a spiritual battle of eternal proportions.

Jesus would not be turned aside, which means that He saw in that cup the bitter dregs of the sin of the world. Jesus saw all that had to be drunk to save us from our sins, and was horrified to see His own face reflected in that cup.

Imagine all the sin of the world in that cup. Jesus saw every evil and vile act, every filthy thought and word, those things that so many wink and laugh at today, and it nearly killed Him on the spot! Jesus realized that on the cross He would be judged guilty of all of that sin—and indeed, He was.

In the place of sinners like you and me, Jesus was judged guilty of murder. He was judged guilty of hatred. He was judged guilty of pride. He was judged guilty of perversion. He was judged guilty of immorality. He was judged guilty of stealing. He was judged guilty of all *our* sins.

Praying in Agony

No wonder the Scripture says our Lord fell under the weight of His agony and cried out to God, "Father, all things are possible for You. Take this cup away from Me" (Mark 14:35–36a). You see, that cup also held the wrath of a holy God, which burns against sin. God must judge sin, even if that judgment falls on His beloved Son.

A Near-Death Experience

Verse 34 indicates that Jesus was near death. In fact, many Bible teachers believe He would have died in Gethsemane had not an angel appeared to strengthen Him (Luke 22:43). We know that it is possible to die from your emotions. It is possible to die of sorrow, grief, anger, fear, or worry.

My father was murdered in 1970. I was a newly married college student at the time, speaking at a youth rally in west Texas when I got a message to call my brother in Ft. Worth. It was urgent. When my brother answered the phone, I asked him what was wrong. "Dad has been hurt," he said.

My wife, Deb, drove from our home in Abilene to pick me up, and we hurried to Ft. Worth. It was there I learned that my father, who managed a hardware store on the east side of the city, had been bludgeoned by a shoplifter. As my dad tried to stop him, the man beat him into unconsciousness with a hammer.

Dad was undergoing brain surgery when Deb and I arrived. For the next ten days, our family virtually lived at the hospital's intensive care unit as Dad lingered. Anyone who has spent time in a hospital waiting for word on a dying loved one knows what it does to you physically and emotionally. Dad never regained consciousness before slipping from this life.

It was not but a few months after his death that my mother began to have chest pains. She had been healthy all of her life. But for the next five years I watched my mother, with her heart broken and grieving for my father, die of loneliness.

As much as my brother and I tried to encourage her and strengthen her, it was to no avail. In my estimation, my mother died of a broken heart.

Drops of Blood

Jesus did not die, but the Gospel of Luke records that something very interesting happened. "His sweat became like great drops of blood falling down to the ground" (Luke 22:44b). This is the condition called chromidrosis, in which the small capillaries under the skin burst and blood oozes through the pores.

In His agony, Jesus' blood became mingled with His sweat and tears as He lay prostrate on His face. Can you picture that? The Lord of glory, with blood pouring from His skin, tears from His eyes, and sweat from His body, lying with His face in the dirt, crying out to God in deep sorrow? It is too much for our minds to comprehend.

"Take This Cup"

In Jesus' final hour there was sorrow, but there was also supplication. He cried, "Abba, Father," that intimate term of a boy to his father, much like we would say "Daddy." He cried "[Daddy], all things are possible for You. Take this cup away from Me; nevertheless, not what I will, but what You will" (Mark 14:36).

Was Jesus praying, "Father, get Me through this hour, get Me through this pain"? Yes, I think His prayer included that. But beyond that, He was calling to His Father, using this term of endearment, because He was feeling overwhelmed. As we have seen, Jesus sought to draw nearer to His Father in intimacy as He felt separated and isolated in the garden.

Jesus was also pleading to God for release, for mercy. He was asking God if there was not some other way He could save the world. He was saying, "Father, if there is any other way to save mankind, let Me do it another way." Jesus was expressing the true feelings of His humanity to God.

You can believe that if there had been any other way for us to be saved, God would have come up with it right there. I am amused when I hear people talking about being saved in some other way, such as by sincere religious belief or good works. If God could have saved us in any other way, don't think for a minute He would not have spared His dear Son right there in Gethsemane.

Surrendering in Obedience

We have also seen that Satan was mightily at work here, tempting the Son of God in His humanity to walk away from the Cross. Jesus' prayer was the crisis point. He knew there was no salvation except by the Cross. God's way and Satan's way lay before Him. Obedience or disobedience was the choice—and He chose obedience!

It is in the final sentence of Jesus' prayer, found in Mark 14:36b, that we find our hope and our joy: "Not what I will, but what You will." Here was full surrender to the Father's will, because sin must be punished. The sacrifice of our Lord was the only payment acceptable for our sin.

If God could have forgiven sin without the shedding of Jesus' blood, then the suffering in Gethsemane and the Cross would have been an act of injustice on God's part, and that is impossible. So in His supplication, Jesus settled the issue and was strengthened to go all the way in obedience.

Lessons from the Garden

We have so much to learn from our Lord as we have witnessed His agony in the garden. The lessons of Gethsemane are ones that will sustain no matter how deep the darkness that engulfs us.

Pour out Your Heart

When you face your dark hour of Gethsemane, it is all right to tell God how you feel. It is all right to pour out the honest agony of your soul to Him. Jesus did.

The writer of Hebrews says our Lord "offered up prayers and supplications, with vehement cries and tears" (Heb. 5:7). God is never surprised or shocked when you cry out in agony to Him. He will never say to you, "I never expected that of you. Shape up!" He understands your hurt and feels your grief.

Watch and Pray

Let me point out another vital lesson for us in the remaining verses of Mark 14:

Then He came and found them sleeping, and said to Peter, "Simon, are you sleeping? Could you not watch one hour? Watch and pray,

lest you enter into temptation. The spirit indeed is willing, but the
flesh is weak."

(Mark 14:37–38)

I call this the episode of the "sleepy saints," as Jesus
returned from praying three times and found the three disciples asleep.

Although the Lord was not surprised by this, I'm certain
it must have added to His grief to know that these three men
could not stay awake in His hour of need. It must have hurt
to know that they were so weak and so insensitive to His
pain that they snored through His agony.

Luke the physician gives us some possible insight into the
sleepiness of Peter, James, and John (Mark 14:39–40). In
Luke 22:45, he says they slept "from sorrow."

Perhaps they were overcome with grief. Perhaps depression caused their fatigue. Maybe they were trying to escape
the reality of what was ahead, and sleep was the only escape.
Maybe they were so deeply disturbed and confused that their
lack of diligence and faithfulness could be excused to some
degree.

Whatever the cause of their drowsiness, Jesus chided them
for not staying awake and praying. Had they prayed, they
would have been given the courage and strength they
needed to face Gethsemane. So Jesus asked them, "Could
you not watch one hour?" (Mark 14:37).

What a message to a sleepy church in our time. What a
message to Christians today who refuse to pray. The message is so clear to us: "Watch and pray, lest you enter into
temptation," because we will face dark hours. We will face
our own Gethsemane and cross experiences.

We need to learn how to pray through the darkness because there will come a time when getting hold of God, and getting an answer to prayer, will be the most important issue in our lives.

So many face the hour of sorrow when their world caves in, and they wonder where God is.

Jesus says to us, "Watch, be prepared, and pray." Don't wait until the last minute to pray. Learn to pray now in preparation, watch and pray so that when the crisis comes, when Gethsemane's darkness falls around you, you'll be strong and courageous and you'll pray through the darkness.

Surrender to God

Jesus would also teach us that prayer is not bending God's will to our will. It is bending our will to His will. When you pray, you may have an idea of what you are praying for, but God may have a better idea. Your idea may not be God's idea at all, or it may not be God's idea for that moment.

Jesus says to us, "When you pray, pray in surrender to the Father." Not only is our flesh weak, but the Bible tells us we don't know what to pray for as we ought (Rom. 8:26).

Surrender to God's will is the only path of wisdom. The way to live a life of victory, even though the flesh is weak and we're sleepy, is to learn the secret of prevailing prayer. When we pray, we are strengthened for victory and made strong to face the enemies of sin and sorrow and Satan.

Jesus taught us to pray, "Do not lead us into temptation, but deliver us from the evil one" (Matt. 6:13). So we learn that prayer enables us to be victorious, and that the heart of prayer is a yieldedness, a surrender of ourselves to God.

If the Son of God needed to pray in His hour of anguish and sorrow, how much more we need to pray always as we face our Gethsemanes. For there is strength in prayer.

Breaking Through the Clouds

Notice how the atmosphere in Gethsemane changes in verses 41–42 of Mark 14 as our Lord wipes the sweat from His brow and the blood from His hands: "Then He came the third time and said to them, 'Are you still sleeping and resting? It is enough! The hour has come; behold, the Son of Man is being betrayed into the hands of sinners. Rise, let us be going. See, My betrayer is at hand.'"

Jesus didn't wait for them to come and arrest Him. He went out to face His betrayer and to meet those who would kill Him. I marvel at the courage and determination of our Lord!

It was because in prayer and brokenness, in darkness and desperation, He experienced the power of God to go on and face His final hour and His final days. He knew that on the other side of the Cross was the empty tomb.

Have you ever had the experience of getting on an airplane when the rain is pouring down and the clouds are all around you? It's dark and very dangerous-looking, and when you take off the plane shudders a little bit as it moves through the dark clouds.

Then comes that moment when you break through the clouds and realize you're in bright sunlight. You look beneath you at the dark clouds you have just passed through, then you look again in amazement at the beautiful sunlight streaming around you.

That is what happens when we pray through the darkness, when we watch and keep awake and maintain our vigil with God. He takes us through the dark clouds and the dark days, and then we gain a new perspective as He takes us up above the darkness into the pure light of His glory.

That's what Jesus saw in Gethsemane. He would drink His cup to its last bitter dregs as He who knew no sin became sin for us. But in the drinking of it, in His perfect submission and obedience to the Father, in His provision of salvation for us, the Lord Jesus Christ looked beyond the garden and the Cross and saw the joy that was set before Him (Heb. 12:2). It was a joy that enabled Him to endure the Cross and despise its shame.

When your Gethsemane comes, in the dark hour and dark night of your soul, I promise you that if you know Christ and if you know the surrender of prayer, you can experience strength and solace and comfort even in the darkest hour. If you will pray through the darkness, God will lift you above and beyond your circumstances into the pure light of His glory.

CHAPTER 10

Miracle at Midnight:
Paul's Earthquake in Jail

Jack Wilcox is a remarkable man with an unusual ministry. I'm thrilled to know him as a friend and fellow servant of Christ as well as a member of our church.

Jack is an ex-professional baseball player, one of the guys who took those all-night bus rides that the minor leagues were famous for in the 1940s. Jack came to Christ about fifteen or twenty years ago, and in the late 1980s started going on prison ministry outreaches.

God touched his heart with the work, and now he is a full-time prison chaplain at the state prison in Huntsville. Every time a prisoner is executed at Huntsville, Jack Wilcox is there. He speaks every day to dying men.

In the spiritual realm, so do we! And if we can help people see that God is real even in the darkness of a prison, we can point them to the One who can give them light.

We are going to walk the corridors of a prison in this chapter. So far our biblical journey has taken us into a couple of very unusual "prisons." We have visited the belly of a great fish with Jonah and spent the night with Daniel in a den of lions.

In this chapter, we will visit a real jail, complete with chains and stocks and locked doors and a jailer. It's in the city of Philippi, and the story is in Acts 16. We are going to see that God is real even when prison doors are slammed shut and locked.

The two men we will meet in this jail are Paul and Silas, who were plunged into a midnight of pain not because of their foolishness, but because of their faithfulness to the Lord Jesus Christ.

So we are right back into the darkness, but I have something wonderful to show you. We're going to see Paul and Silas turn their midnight madness into a miracle of God's grace in the original version of "Jailhouse Rock"!

The Safest Place on Earth

The truth I want you to grasp is this: The safest place on earth is in the center of God's will. No matter where you are or what you are going through, to be in the will of God is to be immortal, for the Scripture says, "He who does the will of God abides forever" (1 John 2:17).

I *cannot* say that the center of God's will is the most comfortable and pain-free place on earth. Sometimes, as in the account before us, we are plunged into the midnight hour not because of any disobedience to God or neglect of our spiritual disciplines or commitments.

On the contrary, we can be walking with God and walk right into the middle of a problem or a painful experience. Remember, God is seeking to perfect our faith and use us to draw others to Himself. His first concern is our holiness, not necessarily our happiness; our conformity to Christ, not necessarily our comfort.

So let's dispel the notion that obedience and faithfulness to Christ guarantee a carefree life. The devil will oppose every effort we make to draw close to Christ or share the gospel. You can count on the fact that if you determine in your heart to be a clear-cut witness for Christ, you will face the devil.

Sometimes Christians say, "I don't seem to have any problem with the devil. I don't ever meet up with him." That could be because those Christians are going the same direction he's going! Any time you take a different direction than the devil, you'll meet him face-to-face.

The Trip to Philippi

Paul and his companion Silas were spreading the gospel on Paul's second missionary journey when the apostle received his famous "Macedonian call" in a night vision (Acts 16:9–10). His conclusion was that "the Lord had called us to preach the gospel to [the Macedonians]" (Acts 16:10).

The Call to Philippi

Don't miss the connection between Paul's vision and his visit to Philippi, which is where I want to pick up the story. We tend to forget that God called Paul and Silas specifically to Philippi, "the foremost city of that part of Macedonia" (Acts 16:12).

This also means God led them into "the middle of the griddle," a fiery trial in Philippi. Paul and Silas became the objects of a terrible injustice perpetrated by cruel and evil men under the direction of Satan himself. And all because of their deep devotion to God and their commitment to sharing the gospel.

The Trouble in Philippi

How did Paul and Silas manage to land in jail in Philippi? It all started when they began aggressively sharing their faith in this Roman colony.

Their first convert in that region was a woman by the name of Lydia, "a seller of purple" (Acts 16:14). This fine, aristocratic lady opened her heart to the Lord, and Paul and his companions led her to Christ. Then she opened her home for the first church there at Philippi.

Later, as Paul and Silas were on their way to worship, the trouble started. A little slave girl began to follow them around day after day. We're told she was possessed with "a spirit of divination" (Acts 16:16), which is psychic powers.

In other words, she was a fortune-teller. This is an age-old satanic practice which, as I said in an earlier chapter, is as current as tonight's cable TV offerings. Nowadays you can call a 900 number and have your fortune told for a fee.

This girl followed Paul and Silas, crying out, "These men are the servants of the Most High God, who proclaim to us the way of salvation" (Acts 16:17). Now that was the right message. Paul and Silas were servants of God, and they were proclaiming the way of salvation.

However, her source was the wrong one. Paul didn't want the devil promoting his message, so he wheeled around and confronted the evil spirit within this girl. He said, "I command you in the name of Jesus Christ to come out of her" (Acts 16:18).

The evil spirit left her "that very hour" (Acts 16:18). This poor girl was delivered from the power and the grip of the enemy, and she became a believer in the Lord Jesus Christ.

What an interesting contrast we have here! Paul's first convert was sensitive, sophisticated Lydia, a leading business-woman in Philippi. His next convert was a girl twice enslaved, to her masters and to Satan, a member of the lower social and economic strata, full of evil powers.

It doesn't matter! The message of Jesus Christ is for anyone, regardless of sophistication or the lack of it. Wherever people may land on the social scale, everyone is a candidate for the life-changing power of Jesus Christ.

Now when this little slave girl came to Christ, her owners had a fit. The text says, "They seized Paul and Silas and dragged them into the marketplace to the authorities" (Acts 16:19).

The men who possessed this girl had used her to make "much profit" for themselves (Acts 16:16). Fortune-telling was a big bucks operation then, just as it is today.

When their "meal ticket" got saved and got rid of her demons, these members of the "Philippian mafia" became infuriated. They dragged Paul and Silas before the court on trumped-up charges: "These men, being Jews, exceedingly trouble our city; and they teach customs which are not lawful for us, being Romans, to receive or observe" (Acts 16:20–21).

The real problem, of course, was not Jewish or Roman customs. The real problem in Philippi was these men who were racketeering and profiteering, trading on the souls of men and women. Paul and Silas weren't the problem.

Doesn't that sound familiar? So many people look at Christians today and say, "These radical Christians are the problem. They're the ones stirring up all the trouble in our schools and in society. We would be all right if they would just keep quiet."

Whenever I hear something like this, I think of the prophet Elijah, who stood before the wicked King Ahab and Queen Jezebel (see Chapter 2). Just before the great contest on Mount Carmel, Elijah met Ahab, who said to him, "Is that you, O troubler of Israel?" (1 Kings 18:17).

Without flinching or stammering, the rawboned prophet looked King Ahab right in the eye and said, "I have not troubled Israel, but you and your father's house have" (1 Kings 18:18). Ahab was an ungodly Baal worshiper. He was the cause of Israel's woes, so Elijah set the record straight.

Let's set the record straight too. The real problem in a community or a nation is not the believers in Jesus Christ, the God-fearing, God-honoring, family-loving, committed people. The real problem is those who put their selfish material gain above the souls of men. These are the ones who trouble us.

The Injustice in Philippi

That was the case in Philippi. Because these men saw their profit going down the drain, they turned on Paul and Silas. What followed was a great injustice.

Paul and Silas were beaten unmercifully with rods, without benefit of trial. Then they were thrown into prison, and the jailer was ordered to "keep them securely." So he put them into the "inner prison" with their feet in stocks (Acts 16:22–24).

This Philippian jailer was no doubt a hardened man, perhaps a retired Roman soldier who now had a job keeping the jail. You might suppose that a man like this would be the least likely to come to Jesus Christ. Wouldn't you think that a cruel, insensitive jailer would be the last person to be saved? He was a mission impossible.

How do we know he was cruel and insensitive? Because he took Paul and Silas—already battered, bloodied, and broken—and threw them into the inner dungeon, down among the rats and the refuse and the darkness of the night.

And as if these battered men might have the strength to escape, he locked their feet in tight and uncomfortable stocks. I'm sure they had chains hanging on them too. Can you picture this incredible scene?

Here are these great men of God, men destined for glory, carrying out legendary missionary service. Now they sit in a dark dungeon, beaten and bloodied, hung out to dry and to die. Do you suppose that just once, *Why is this happening to us?* might have entered their minds?

Do you suppose Paul and Silas questioned whether they were in the will of God? Do you think maybe some doubt crept into their hearts as they looked around and said, "Perhaps we shouldn't have come here"?

I don't think so! These men were in the center of God's will, and they knew it. They were strong. This was "wimp-free" Christianity. These men were tough, ready to pay a price for following Christ. The Christian life is no place for cowards.

Praise in the Jail

So here is the situation in the Philippian jail, and that brings us to Acts 16:25. I love this verse, because it turns the whole story around with these words: "But at midnight Paul and Silas were praying and singing hymns to God."

A Song Service

Excuse me, Luke. Did you say they were *singing*? Was there some kind of a song service going on in that prison? There was indeed, in just about the last place on earth you would expect to hear the first sacred concert ever in Europe!

I'm sure that many men had cursed in that prison. I have no doubt that many had blasphemed God there. But none had ever sung praises to God before Paul and Silas arrived.

Did you notice when this praise service broke out? It was at midnight when Paul and Silas turned their pain into a pulpit. They began praising God, and they had an audience. The latter part of verse 25 says "the prisoners were listening to them."

That doesn't mean the other prisoners were merely amused by these singing saints. The language conveys the idea that they were listening to Paul and Silas with rapt attention.

We're not told here, but I have a suspicion that Paul was able to lead many of those prisoners to faith in Jesus Christ. Paul and Silas may have been praying and singing for some time before the earthquake hit.

I believe some of the prisoners heard those songs in the night and called out to Paul and Silas, "What are you guys doing? How can you sing like that? Tell us what you've got that we haven't got."

An Earthquake

Not only were Paul and Silas playing to a rapt house, but their praying and singing brought the house down! Prayer and praise are powerful weapons in the hand of God. An earthquake struck in the middle of this midnight praise service, shaking the prison doors open and breaking all the prisoners' chains.

I like to think that Silas sang tenor, Paul sang monotone, and God joined in on the bass and shook that place until it rumbled and rattled. This was a miracle for sure, but the real miracle is the way God transformed that prison into a platform:

> *And the keeper of the prison, awaking from sleep and seeing the prison doors open, supposing the prisoners had fled, drew his sword and was about to kill himself. But Paul called with a loud voice, saying, "Do yourself no harm, for we are all here."*
>
> (Acts 16:27–28)

The jailer may have just shook his head and rolled over when he heard those crazy Christians singing down there in the dungeon. But the earthquake definitely got his attention.

Guards in those days were responsible for their prisoners. We'll see in Chapter 11, about the shipwreck of Acts 27, that the guards planned to kill Paul and the other prisoners rather than risk them escaping. The law of the day was that if you were in charge of prisoners and they escaped on your watch, you died (see also Acts 12:18–19).

The jailer was in a suicidal panic by the time he got fully awake and realized what had happened. Isn't it interesting that after Paul reassured him his prisoners had not escaped, he ran in and fell trembling before Paul and Silas? He was drawn like a magnet to these Christians in the midst of his crisis.

The Jailer's Salvation

Then this jailer asked the greatest of all questions in Acts 16:30: "Sirs, what must I do to be saved?" He was saying, "How can a man like me be saved?"

Note that Paul, one of the great theologians of all time, didn't give this man a lecture on the doctrine of salvation.

He didn't talk about the sovereign will of God. He just said so simply and sublimely, "Believe on the Lord Jesus Christ, and you will be saved" (Acts 16:31).

Is the doctrine of salvation important? Of course it is. Is the sovereign will of God an indispensable element in salvation? Absolutely. Verse 32 tells us that Paul and Silas had an opportunity to share the gospel with the jailer and his family, and I'm sure they expounded the truth in more detail. My point is that this man did not need to be sold on the product!

He was obviously repentant. He was trembling and broken. He had already despaired of his life. Acts 16:31 captures the beauty and the utter simplicity of salvation. Someone has said that if we just supply the sinner, God will supply the Savior.

That is exactly what happened to the Philippian jailer. He put his trust in Jesus Christ and received Him by faith as his Lord and Savior. He was saved on the spot. His salvation was immediate and total. And not only that, his whole household came to Christ, obviously following his lead.

How do we know he was saved?

For one thing, the jailer acted differently. He took Paul and Silas out of the dungeon and began to wash the bloody wounds on their backs. "And he took them the same hour of the night and washed their stripes." More important, "he and all his family were baptized. Now when he had brought them into his house, he set food before them; and he rejoiced, having believed in God with all his household" (Acts 16:33–34).

Baptism is a step of obedience and identification with Christ that we tend to take for granted, but it could be costly in the first-century world. Verse 34 is especially interesting because it says the Philippian jailer shared his food with the two missionaries, a reminder of the breaking of bread in fellowship that was a trademark of the early church.

Don't hurry over that little phrase, "he rejoiced." The praise and worship hadn't ended. It had just changed locations! In fact, I can just hear the jailer saying to Paul and Silas, "What was that song you were singing earlier about Jesus? Will you teach it to me?"

I don't know if this jailer could carry a tune on his key ring, but can you imagine the racket as these three men, backed by the jailer's family, lifted their voices in loud and joyous praise to God?

What an experience! What an earth-shaking, earth-quaking, spiritual experience happened in that Philippian jailhouse. It was truly a miracle at midnight.

Your Miracle at Midnight

What is significant about midnight? It's the deepest hour of the night. Why? Because one second after midnight, it's officially morning.

I suspect you have been in many a midnight hour. I have, not only in my own life, but in the lives of the people to whom God has called me to minister. Through the years I've walked with some families into a darkness so deep there was seemingly no way through it.

I have walked down the darkened corridors of a hospital intensive care unit with a family experiencing a midnight hour. I have stood in the hushed halls of a funeral home, in a hospital room, or in a home with believers when darkness shrouded their lives and they thought the sun would never shine again.

Just recently, I made such a journey with a family in our church whose precious little girl slipped from here into eternity. I huddled with those grieving parents as they said goodbye to their daughter for the last time.

Let me tell you, you cannot walk through the darkness with a family like that and ever be the same. The Spanish proverb says, "There is never a home without its hush."

Never the Final Word

I want you to know that with Jesus Christ, the darkness and the hush are never the final word. I have watched so many men and women of God like these parents who have had a song in the night, a testimony of faith in the darkest night of their lives.

The world looks at this and asks, "How can these things be?" How could Paul and Silas sing in that dark, dank jail when they were locked down and their backs oozed with blood?

They could sing because their joy wasn't in circumstances. It certainly was not in that jail. Their joy was in Jesus. Paul would later write to the believers at Philippi, "The things which happened to me have actually turned out for the furtherance of the gospel" (Phil. 1:12). Then he concluded that if Christ is preached, "in this I rejoice" (v. 18).

Do you want joy like that? Then it needs to be in Someone who will never leave you or forsake you. If your joy is in your health, when your health is gone your joy will be gone. If your joy is in your spouse, when your spouse is taken your joy will be gone. If your joy is in your job, when your job is taken your joy will be gone.

But if your joy is in the Lord Jesus Christ, it can never be taken away from you. Your joy is forever. "In Your presence is fullness of joy; / At Your right hand are pleasures forevermore" writes the psalmist (Ps. 16:11).

A Prayer and Song at Midnight

Do you have a prayer for the midnight hour? Do you have a song to sing that will pierce the darkness? Again, the psalmist David says in Psalm 119:62, "At midnight I will rise to give thanks to You."

You see, anyone can sing in the daylight. It's easy to sing when the sun is shining and everything is going our way. The world has lots of songs for those occasions.

To have a song in the night, to be able to say, "O God, I praise You even in the darkness of this hour," requires more than a sunny disposition. It requires a commitment to worship and praise God even in the midnight of your soul.

The wonderful thing is that when you praise God, even prison walls can't separate you from His presence. The darkest night you can imagine cannot hide the glorious face of God when you praise Him. Through prayer and praise, Paul and Silas found a song in the night.

Psalm 77:6 speaks of that song in the night. Some of the sweetest songs of the Christian faith have been composed in the darkness. I think of Fanny Crosby, perhaps America's greatest hymn writer.

Fanny Crosby was blinded shortly after birth due to an error in judgment on the part of a physician. And yet, out of her blindness she wrote songs like, "Blessed assurance, Jesus is mine! O what a foretaste of glory divine!" (Fanny Crosby, "Blessed Assurance," © 1976, Paragon Associates, Inc.).

Out of the darkness often come the sweetest refrains and the sweetest songs. Why? Because the Christian, even in darkness, can rise above circumstances. The joy of Jesus remains in spite of our present condition.

Blessing out of Bruises

We Christians need to be able to sing at the midnight hour if our testimony is to ring true. Many times, people who won't listen to you as you share your faith are still watching your faithfulness to Jesus.

If you can sing at midnight, you'll be the first one they come to when the darkness envelopes them, just like the jailer who ran trembling to Paul and Silas. He ran to these men because they knew how to turn their pain into a pulpit to proclaim the good news of Jesus Christ.

Do you want to turn life's bruises and bloody wounds into benefit to you and blessing to the cause of Christ? Submit your midnight experiences to the Lord, and surrender to His will.

Then, no matter how dark the night or how harsh the pain, God will give you a song at midnight. And He will give you a miracle at midnight by using your pain and struggles to reach people for Himself that you could never have imagined reaching.

CHAPTER 11

Defeating the Darkness:
SURVIVING A SHIPWRECK

On November 23, 1892, the great evangelist Dwight L. Moody and his son, Will, boarded the ocean liner *Spree* at Southampton, England, for the voyage home to America. Moody had just completed a series of meetings in Great Britain, and he was eager to see his family and the students at his Bible school again.

On the third morning of the trip, the passengers were startled by a loud crash. The shaft of the ship had broken, and the *Spree* began to drift helplessly. The seas were so rough the crew realized the small lifeboats were useless. So they gathered everyone in the ship's main saloon to wait and hope that they would be discovered by a passing ship.

On the second night of this nerve-racking wait, Moody led a prayer service that calmed many of the passengers, including himself. Although he was sure of heaven, the thought of his work ending and of never seeing his family again had unsettled him. I can identify with that!

The next morning, the steamer *Lake Huron* discovered the stranded ship and towed it a thousand miles to safety. The sentiments of the rescued passengers and crew are not recorded, but I suspect they were very glad to have someone on board who knew God and knew how to pray.

A Long-Lasting Storm

When it comes to the storm and shipwreck of Acts 27, I *know* the passengers and crew were glad to have someone like that on board. The storm of Acts 27 was different from the others we have studied because it lasted not only for one dark night, but for many.

In addition, this time the ship was lost. What do you do when night after night after night, there seems to be no hope? We're going to see that even in this kind of circumstance, the glorious presence of God is always there.

Heading Toward the Storm

The apostle Paul found himself, along with 275 other people, on a ship sailing for Rome. Paul was a prisoner on his way to appeal his case before Caesar, for he had been arrested for the proclamation of the gospel of Christ. What the captain and crew didn't know was that they were heading straight toward a terrible storm.

In one sense, Paul was a prisoner of circumstances. He was in chains, thrust into the darkness and into this storm through no fault of his own. Yet even though others around him victimized this man by their foolish and fleshly decisions, the apostle maintained his faith, his confidence, and his courage even when the lights went out.

The entire twenty-seventh chapter of Acts describes this very powerful story. Let's pick up the narrative at verse 13 so we can get a feel for what was happening. Paul's traveling companion Luke writes:

When the south wind blew softly, supposing that they had obtained their desire, putting out to sea, they sailed close by Crete. But not long after, a tempestuous head wind arose, called Euroclydon. So when the ship was caught, and could not head into the wind, we let her drive.

(Acts 27:13–15)

The following verses give a lot of nautical detail that is important, but which you can read for yourself. I want to pick up the text again after the severity of the storm had become apparent. By this time, "all hope that we would be saved was finally given up" (Acts 27:20).

Then Luke records that Paul took over, encouraging the others just as D. L. Moody did that cold November on the high seas:

I urge you to take heart, for there will be no loss of life among you, but only of the ship. For there stood by me this night an angel of the God to whom I belong and whom I serve, saying, "Do not be afraid, Paul; you must be brought before Caesar; and indeed God has granted you all those who sail with you." Therefore take heart, men, for I believe God that it will be just as it was told me."

(Acts 27:22–25)

What a powerful faith Paul possessed! Here, even though he was a prisoner, he ended up the captain of the ship. Because of his faith, because of his courage, because of his confidence in Almighty God, he brought light on a dark night and a dark day.

Thrust into the Storm

Of course, Paul was not the only believer to hit a storm. We enter the storms of life too, sometimes because of our own selfish or sinful choices.

Remember our study of Jonah (Chapter 5)? Here was a man who ran from the will of God and found himself in the midst of a horrifying storm. Jonah has a lot of relatives today, because we often find ourselves in the middle of crises through our own willful disobedience to God.

There are other times when, like Paul, we find ourselves thrust into a storm because of the foolish decisions of others. Turn back a few verses earlier to Acts 27:9 and you will discover that Paul tried to convince those in command of the voyage not to set sail.

The centurion in charge of the prisoners "was more persuaded by the helmsman and the owner of the ship than by the things spoken by Paul" (Acts 27:11). These men were itching to get going regardless of the weather. There were prisoners to deliver and money to be made on the cargo.

So the sailors and the centurion put their heads together. Since the harbor was not suitable for winter (Acts 27:12), they took a vote, and the majority decided they wanted to set sail. An impulsive decision was made to head for a suitable winter harbor.

In other words, these men did what was comfortable and convenient for them, despite Paul's warning in verse 10 that their decision could cost many lives. So as a result of someone else's foolish and impetuous decision, Paul was carried along and carried right into the storm.

Modern-Day Storms

We are living in a time when many people are victims of the choices of others. There are adults living in a storm today because of abuse they suffered as children. Others are facing a storm of difficulties and damaged emotions as the result of a lifetime of victimization. These are people who are suffering through no fault of their own.

I realize our society has become far too "victim conscious." We need to be very careful about always claiming that we're victims of someone else's actions. We need to take responsibility for our lives and our choices.

The fact remains that many people today find themselves in a dark night because of selfish choices made by parents, children, or perhaps a faithless spouse. And often those choices are made in spite of warnings about the dire consequences.

The apostle Paul attempted to persuade the centurion and the sailors, but they probably only laughed at him. In the middle of this storm the apostle had some timely warnings and some answers to give, but no one would listen to him.

You know, things haven't changed much today. Not only individuals, but our nation and the world, are sailing toward a storm like no storm we have ever seen before. Our job as Christians is to try and give warning to people about this approaching storm called Armageddon.

Many Christians today are trying to warn of this destructive storm and the evil sweeping across our world. We know that the answer to all of the darkness, all of the suffering, and all of the heartache is the Word of God and the gospel of Jesus Christ.

When we talk to people we're often ignored—just as Paul's warnings were brushed aside when he tried to warn the sailors. The world plunges on recklessly without Christ, and as a result of the decisions of others, we're riding into the storm ourselves. We're already feeling the leading edge of the storm in our own society because people won't listen to the men and the women of God.

Yet it's interesting to me that when a crisis hits, the world often comes running to the church or running to Christians for answers. When war broke out in the Persian Gulf in 1991, the church I pastor in Dallas and churches across America began filling up. When the bombs started dropping, people came looking for answers.

Because Operation Desert Storm was war in the Middle East, many were asking, "Is this Armageddon? Is this the end of the age?" People were wringing their hands and filling up church services and prayer meetings. But when the bombs stopped dropping, people started dropping out on God.

We who know Christ know that politicians aren't the solution to the world's problems. The environmentalists don't have the answer. The United Nations does not have the answer. God and His people have the answer! No matter whether people listen or not we must keep telling the truth, for one of these days the storm is going to hit.

In Paul's case, God preserved the entire crew, all 276 people on board that ship, because of one person who had faith in God. Did you know that God has given this present world a preservation factor, which is the Church of the Lord Jesus Christ? God's people are salt. We are light.

The Certainty of the Storm

One day, God's people are going to be taken out via the rapture of the church. And then all hell is going to break loose as the Tribulation comes.

The Bible says that the great and mighty, as well as the weak and the poor, are going to huddle in the caves and hide under the rocks and pray for the rocks and the mountains to fall on them and hide them from God's wrath.

It's going to be a rock concert bigger than Woodstock when they start praying that! When the judgment of God falls and the wrath of the Lamb is unleashed against an ungodly, unbelieving world, the storm will have come in all of its fury. But until then, God has placed you and me in this world that we might be salt and light. This does not mean, however, that we are exempt from life's storms.

The fact is that none of us go through life without storms. They are sure to come, just as Paul warned the sailors in Acts 27. Whether you are in the calm before the storm, in the middle of a storm, or just coming out of a storm, the next storm is on its way.

The Word of God tells us we will face dark nights. Jesus Himself said, "In the world you will have tribulation" (John 16:33). Keep reading, though, because Jesus went on to say, "But be of good cheer, I have overcome the world." What a word of hope!

The Suddenness of the Storm

We need this hope because the storms come so suddenly. Look at verse 14 of Acts 27: "Not long after, a tempestuous head wind arose." Paul's warning was still ringing in those sailors' ears when the storm hit.

Scholars have examined verse 14 to determine exactly what kind of wind this was. Luke's use of the Greek word translated "arose" gives indication that he was alluding to some kind of gigantic typhoon.

Whatever it was, it came suddenly and with great power. This storm was so violent that it drove the ship away from the shore. The crew had no control over the ship, and they were enveloped in darkness. Day after day they saw no sun, no light of any kind.

Have you ever been plunged into a storm like that? Maybe it was financial loss, a bad report from the doctor, upheaval in your marriage, the heartbreak of a wayward child, or parents who do not walk with God. Whatever your storm, I want you to imagine for the next few moments that you are on this ship with the apostle Paul.

The sky all around you is filled with darkness. There is no light anywhere. Your ship is being driven and battered, and you are utterly helpless to do anything about it. And you're asking, "Is there any hope?" It's so dark and so dangerous that even these veteran sailors have given up.

Then right in the middle of this terrible darkness, Paul stands on the deck. Everybody is wondering what this crazy little missionary is doing. Paul says, "Take heart, boys! Cheer up!"

Paul has to chide them just a little bit for not listening to him. He says, "I told you so. I told you this was going to happen" (Acts 27:21). But then he urges all of you on board to take heart.

Why? Because he says, "There stood by me this night an angel of the God to whom I belong and whom I serve, saying, 'Do not be afraid, Paul'" (Acts 27:23–24a). Imagine Paul standing there on that deck in the darkness, praising God. His witness for Christ, his message of hope and confidence in God, is a light in your dark night.

The Savior in the Storm

People today are still asking, "Is there any hope?" Our world is full of people clinging to the railing as the storms of life batter them, and they're wondering if they will ever see the light again.

Paul was in a situation like that, yet when the storm was at its worst, he was at his best. How was he able to stand there and say confidently, "Take heart. Don't be afraid"? Because he knew that no matter how terrible the storm and how deep the darkness, the Lord Jesus was with him. Paul belonged to God (Acts 27:23), and that was all that mattered.

I'm telling you, my friend, when the storm hits—and it *will* hit—when the darkness comes, when you're in the middle of a storm, the most important thing in all the world is for you to know that God is with you. The most important truth you can know is that your Savior is standing beside you in the storm.

You will need to cling to that truth when your employer calls you in and says, "I'm sorry, but we're downsizing. We're going to have to let you go."

You will need to know the Lord is with you when the doctor looks at you and says, "I'm sorry. It's cancer."

You will need the reality and the hope of Christ's presence when that telephone call breaks the stillness of the night and a voice on the other end says, "There's been an accident."

Do you know the presence of God? Do you realize that if you know Christ as your Savior, you are *never* alone? In those dark moments of life there's something there you can't explain or describe, but you know it's the presence of God. And you know it's real. He gives the "peace of God, which surpasses all understanding" (Phil. 4:7). You discover the reality of His promise that He will "never leave you nor forsake you" (Heb. 13:5).

Notice the source of Paul's peace. It came from "the God to whom I belong and whom I serve" (Acts 27:23). How do we know that God will never leave us? Because He takes care of His own possessions! What a beautiful picture of a believer resting in his Savior.

The People of the Savior

The Bible is filled with descriptions of believers and our relationship to God. For example, we are called the bride of Christ. That means we are married to Him. He chose us, and has taken us for His own. And a faithful husband He is, who will never forsake His bride.

We are also called in Scripture the sheep of His pasture. Jesus said, "My sheep hear My voice" (John 10:27). Now have you ever wondered why Jesus called us sheep? It's not exactly flattering. Sheep aren't very bright. They have a propensity for wandering off and getting lost. Sheep are also very vulnerable to predators, and are easy prey for those who would attack.

It's not all that great a compliment to be called aimless, wandering sheep, easily led astray. "All we like sheep have gone astray," the prophet Isaiah said. "We have turned, every one, to his own way" (Isa. 53:6).

If we're Christ's sheep, we can call to Him because He's listening for us and hears our faintest cry. And if even one little lamb is lost out of a hundred, He goes and seeks until He finds it, and cares for that one precious little lamb who's lost (Luke 15:4–5). That's the God to whom Paul belonged, and to whom we belong.

God also calls us His children. Now if my children were ever missing, I wouldn't rest until I had found them. If my children are in trouble or are hurting in any way, I do everything within my power to help them.

If as a sinful, erring, and finite father I care that much for my children, think how much more the God who is neither sinful nor erring nor finite cares for us as His children. We have an infinite, loving God who hears us cry even in the darkest night and is there with us!

Finally, the Bible says we are the possession of God. In 1 Corinthians 6:19–20, Paul writes:

> *Do you not know that your body is the temple of the Holy Spirit who is in you . . . and you are not your own? For you were bought at a price.*

We are God's possession, bought with the precious blood of Christ. As I said above, God takes care of His possessions. No wonder Paul could stand in the middle of that storm and say, "I belong to God, and He is going to take care of me."

When I was a young person, we used to sing this little chorus: "I belong to the God of the mountains. I belong to the God of the sea. I belong to the God of the universe. And He belongs to me."

Do you need a word of hope today in the midst of your storm? You belong to God! You are His own! And He will take care of you. Someone has said of Christ:

> To the artist, He's the Altogether Lovely.
> To the baker, He's the Bread of Life.
> To the banker, He's the Hidden Treasure.
> To the biologist, He's the Life.
> To the builder, He's the Chief Cornerstone.
> To the doctor, He's the Great Physician.

To the educator, He's the Truth.

To the farmer, He's the Lord of the harvest.

To the florist, He's the Rose of Sharon.

To the geologist, He's the Rock of Ages.

To the jurist, He's the Righteous Judge.

To the jeweler, He's the Pearl of great price.

To the lawyer, He's the Advocate.

To the publisher, He's the Good News.

To the philosopher, He's the Wisdom of God.

To the preacher, He's the Word of God.

To the sculptor, He's the Living Stone.

To the statesman, He's the Desire of all nations.

To the theologian, He's the Author and Finisher of our faith.

To the traveler, He's the New and the Living Way.

And to the sinner, He's the Lamb of God who takes away the sin of the world.

(author unknown)

Jesus Christ our Lord and our Savior! And to the storm-tossed saint, He says, "I am with you always."

The Promise in the Storm

Since we left Paul in the middle of his storm, let's go back to Acts 27 and find out what happened. After he stood on the ship's deck and announced his faith in God and confidence that everyone on board would be spared, Paul said in Acts 27:25: "I believe God that it will be just as it was told me."

There's more to Paul's confidence here than just the angel's word. Turn back to Acts 23, where Paul is fighting for his very life in Jerusalem. His speech before the

Sanhedrin caused such an uproar that the Roman commander had to send in his troops to rescue Paul and keep him from being torn to pieces (Acts 23:9–10).

Now look at verse 11: "But the following night the Lord stood by him and said, 'Be of good cheer, Paul; for as you have testified for Me in Jerusalem, so you must also bear witness at Rome.'"

The reason Paul could say "Have faith" in the middle of that storm was not just because he was an optimist. No, he had God's promise that he was going to make it to Rome and witness for Him there.

So even though Paul boarded that ship as a prisoner of circumstances, even though the ship was driven by the wind, even though it was dark all day and all night for days on end, even though it seemed that there was no hope, Paul had a sure word from God, and he hung on to it even in the storm.

We have the sure Word of God too. We have His promises. Therefore, we can know that no matter the circumstance, we are in the plan and the purpose of God, and we are homeward bound. Nothing should be able to separate us from His love, which is in Christ Jesus.

And as long as we are in the will of God, we are safe and secure. We are walking in His presence. We are living by His promises. We are as sure of heaven as if we were already there, and in the meantime, we have confidence and courage since there is no reason to fear.

The Ruler of the Storm

This kind of person always rises to the top because no centurion or sailor or ship owner can ever circumvent the plan of God. He is sovereign.

And even when God didn't rule as these men disobeyed Him and took Paul with them, God *over*ruled their plans. "And we know that all things work together for good to those who love God, to those who are the called [literally, who "fit in"] according to His purpose" (Rom. 8:28).

God uses strange circumstances sometimes to save His own. One of my predecessors at the First Baptist Church of West Palm Beach, Florida, was Dr. Jess Moody. On one occasion, Jess and several young ministerial students boarded a small aircraft to go to a preaching engagement Jess had somewhere.

On the way back, the plane's landing gear wouldn't release. The pilot sent word back to Jess and his boys: "We've got a problem. The landing gear won't come down. We've tried everything." Now if you can't get that front landing gear down, that means a possible crash. So do you know what they did?

The pilot radioed the airport and was advised to circle until he had emptied the gasoline tanks. That way if there was a crash, the fuel wouldn't explode. So here was Jess and his college preacher boys circling around and around over West Palm Beach. It took more than an hour to empty the tanks of fuel.

You can imagine that in that amount of time, fear can set in quite easily. So while they were circling and running out of gas, Jess and the preacher boys were praying.

Suddenly, Jess had an idea. Now he's a rather large man, so he said, "Guys, let's get to the back of the plane." So they all went to the back of the airplane, got on their knees, and somehow managed to strap themselves in. Then they had a prayer meeting.

In the meantime, the word had got out that Dr. Jess Moody's plane might crash. So the news cameras and the local radio and television stations were there at the airport waiting for them. The foam was on the runway. The plane came sliding in with no explosion and no crash, a safe landing.

When Jess got off the plane a reporter from Miami stuck a microphone in his face and asked, "Dr. Moody, what happened? What did you do?"

Jess described how they got to the back of that plane and what they did. Then, pointing to his stomach he said, "We came in on the wings of prayer and the miracle of obesity!"

God can use any circumstance and condition to accomplish His purpose—whether it's a big preacher or a big storm! We do our part. He does His part.

The Light After the Darkness

Paul was destined for Rome. You see, the books of Ephesians and Colossians and 2 Timothy and all the others were on that boat, still in the heart of Paul waiting to be written. God wasn't finished with him yet. So Paul and his companions were saved and the day broke, because one man in the night had faith in God, because one man in the night was God's light.

> Jesus Savior, pilot me,
> Over life's tempestuous sea.
> Unknown waves before me roll,
> Hiding rocks and treacherous shoals.
> Chart and compass come from Thee,
> Jesus Savior, pilot me.
>
> (J. E. Gould, *Jesus, Savior, Pilot Me*)

If you can sing that even in the darkest night of your soul, you will never be without hope. If you can sing those words, no shipwreck will be able to wreck your confidence in God.

CHAPTER 12

No Night There:
THE JOY OF HEAVEN

I guess the title of this chapter gives away the punch line, doesn't it? We have no more night scenes to consider, because our final subject is heaven, our eternal home, the land of endless day and endless light.

During my recent trip to Israel, which I mentioned earlier, our group was assigned a wonderful tour guide for our visit to the garden tomb. He was actually a believer from Great Britain who had retired in Israel. He was a delight and a blessing as he led us through an inspiring tour of the garden tomb.

Well, we have a tour guide for this chapter, the best one possible. He's John, the beloved apostle of Jesus Christ, who is going to guide us through the new Jerusalem as we enter the portals of heaven and walk the streets of glory. Our "map" for the tour is Revelation 21–22, God's final word to His people.

It is noteworthy that John would describe the end of the very concept of night and darkness. He was an aged man by the time he wrote the book of Revelation under the inspiration of the Holy Spirit. The shadows of death were gathering around him.

What's more, John wrote from exile on a forsaken island called Patmos, the "devil's island" of its time. No doubt John spent many long, dark nights on that island, separated from family and friends, longing for heaven with a faraway look in his eye.

I am sure he spent many hours remembering his time with Jesus, three brief years that changed his life forever. Perhaps John thought that his ministry was over, that he would live out his days in exile and then go home to see his beloved Savior.

The New Heaven and New Earth

The risen Jesus Christ was not through using His humble disciple. For there on Patmos John had a phenomenal experience. He was permitted by the Spirit of God to look down the corridors of time and record the events of the final days of human history.

Walking into Heaven

It is as though John boarded a divine time machine and rode through eternity, and then God permitted him to report to us the sights and the sounds and the scenes of the life to come. What John recorded for us in Revelation is what he saw and experienced when he came face-to-face with the glory of God, and was allowed to walk in the presence of God in heaven itself.

At least a dozen times in Revelation, John was commanded to write what he saw or heard. The final command is in Revelation 21:5, following the first portion of the apostle's breathtaking account of what it is going to be like in heaven:

"And God will wipe away every tear from their eyes; there shall be
no more death, nor sorrow, nor crying. There shall be no more pain,
for the former things have passed away." Then He who sat on the
throne said, "Behold, I make all things new." And He said to me,
"Write, for these words are true and faithful."

(Rev. 21:4–5)

This is the "new heaven" and "new earth" John saw (v. 1) by the revelation of the Holy Spirit. Imagine what it was like for him to see a vision like this, record it for all believers, and then face another interminably long and lonely night on his island prison.

John probably didn't sleep very well. He tossed and turned, trying to make a rock into a pillow. With the sun hidden and the darkness creeping in, John was subject to the cold air and the animals that would roam about.

Often in the evening we have the opportunity for quiet conversation with friends, but not so for John. He had no friends with whom to share his evenings, no companion to drive away the chill of the night. All he had was pitch darkness every night.

The End of Darkness

As John began to describe the beauty and the joys of heaven, however, surely his spirit revived as he wrote of the believer's heavenly home. The description begins in earnest in Revelation 21:10, and some stunning verses follow.

But notice in particular verse 25, where John records that the gates of the new Jerusalem "shall not be shut at all by day." Then, as if expecting the obvious question, "What about at night?" the apostle adds parenthetically, "There shall be no night there."

I have to wonder if it was night when the Holy Spirit inspired John to write those words. Perhaps John put down his quill or whatever he was using and tried to comprehend what had just been revealed to him.

It is hard for us to comprehend it even today. "No night there." No more darkness for the Christian! My friend, heaven is not a dream. And because of heaven, life need no longer be a nightmare.

Heaven, the Ultimate Reality

Heaven is the ultimate reality for the children of God. It is the bright hope of our hearts in an otherwise increasingly dark world. The apostle Paul wasn't about to abandon his hope of heaven: "If in this life only we have hope in Christ, we are of all men the most pitiable" (1 Cor. 15:19).

Georgie Jessel was delivering the eulogy at the funeral of fellow performer Gracie Allen, the late wife of comedian George Burns, who himself died in early 1996 at the age of one hundred.

Jessel said, "The hope of mankind must be in the faith that the play is never over. When the curtain falls, it rises again. If we don't believe this, then this has all been a big gag and the punch line is futility."

Jessel was right. If there is no life beyond, if there is no life after life and no hope of heaven, then all becomes futile and meaningless. This is what Solomon meant when he said of life under the sun, life lived merely on a horizontal plane, "Vanity of vanities, all is vanity" (Eccl. 1:2).

The Source of Life's Purpose

If this life is to mean anything, we must have a purpose for living. What greater purpose can there be than to live for the promise of a place where there will be no more night, no more despair, no more doubt, no more fear, no more failure, no more sin, no more suffering, and no more heartache?

Is thinking about heaven "pie in the sky, by-and-by"? Definitely not. The people who do the most in this life are those who think most about the next life. Those who have their hearts set on heaven, their eyes focused upon what is to come, do the most in the life that is now.

The difference is that for the Christian, this cosmos—this temporary, material world—is not all there is. You see, God has made us for eternity. Solomon also wrote in Ecclesiastes, "He has put eternity in [our] hearts" (3:11).

There is a desire within us for heaven, implanted by God Himself. In this, mankind is alone among God's creation. The animals have no inclination toward heaven. But God has so created you and me that we know He is there, and that beyond this life is the life to come.

As believers we experience eternal life even now, which means that life as we know it today is just a warm-up, a preparation for that which is to come. If you are a believer in the Lord Jesus Christ, heaven should be in your heart every day. It should be the passion and the driving purpose of your life.

Our Eternal Destination

What would it be like to live in the darkness of doubt all of your days? What would it be like to live without any sense of purpose or any destination to set your hopes on?

Well, I imagine it would be like boarding an airplane for your dream vacation to, say, Paris. Suppose you are on such a flight when, about halfway over the Atlantic Ocean, the pilot comes on the intercom with this announcement:

"You're welcome to unfasten your seat belts and get as comfortable as you like. Feel free to walk about the cabin. We're going to serve you a great meal soon, so enjoy it. I want you to enjoy the flight, but I do need to tell you that we have no destination.

"That's right, we're not really going to Paris. As a matter of fact, we're just going to circle the Atlantic Ocean until we run out of fuel and fall into the water."

Imagine hearing that. You thought you were on your way to Paris for the vacation of a lifetime. This trip had meaning. Your ticket showed a destination. But as soon as the destination is taken away and you realize you're just circling and going down, then despair and hopelessness set in.

Such it is in life. If all you're doing is circling, just existing without purpose and hope until you run out of fuel and go down, then life becomes absolutely dreadful and miserable.

The Scripture says we are designed to reach an eternal destination. It is the knowledge that I am on my way to heaven that makes me want to get up every day and do something productive for Jesus until the day I stand before Him.

Heaven is not a form of escapism. It is not "pie in the sky, by-and-by." Heaven is a present reality to the believer, and the longer we live the more homesick for heaven we become.

Paul said toward the end of his life, "For to me, to live is Christ, and to die is gain. . . . For I am hard pressed between the two, having a desire to depart and be with Christ, which is far better" (Phil. 1:21, 23).

A Description of Heaven

So John describes our heavenly home in Revelation 21 and 22. Now remember that the apostle John is describing heaven after the long nights of tribulation and war and famine and distress that are described in the earlier chapters of Revelation.

We have already briefly considered chapter 21, so I want to look at the opening verses of Revelation 22, with which John climaxes his description of heaven:

> [He] showed me a pure river of water of life, clear as crystal, proceeding from the throne of God and of the Lamb. In the middle of its street, and on either side of the river, was the tree of life, which bore twelve fruits, each tree yielding its fruit every month. And the leaves of the tree were for the healing of the nations.
>
> (vv. 1–2)

There is more in these and the following verses than we can understand in a lifetime of study. It is as though after the smoke of tribulation and judgment clears, there stands before John the indescribable beauty of heaven.

Our future home is much more than the mind can comprehend and the tongue can explain—but it is glorious to make the effort.

I feel like a Little Leaguer stepping up to bat in Yankee Stadium when I try to describe the glories of heaven. And yet, John tells us that those who read and contemplate the Revelation have a special blessing from God (Rev. 1:3).

Everlasting Light

Even though heaven is more wonderful than anything we can imagine, I want to consider the Bible's final picture of heaven in these final pages of our study together.

Look at Revelation 22:5: "There shall be no night there: They need no lamp nor light of the sun, for the Lord God gives them light. And they shall reign forever and ever." Do you see it again, the same phrase we saw above in Revelation 21:25?

"There shall be no night there," John tells us. All the glories of heaven will be illuminated in everlasting light; not by a burning fireball called the sun, but by the glory of the eternal God.

A Real Place

And so John begins in Revelation 22:1 to describe some of the features of the "holy city, New Jerusalem" (Rev. 21:2). Now let me stop here and underline this truth for you once again. Heaven is not a state of mind. It is not some kind of supernatural "cyberspace," nor is it wispy, ethereal, or vaporous.

Heaven is a real place that exists in a time and a dimension beyond this world and this life. It is the land where the shadows of death will be banished forever (Rev. 21:4).

What a wonderful promise! Down here, death is the ultimate darkness, the final night, the last enemy with whom to be dealt. But we have it all backward.

Dr. Howard Hendricks says, "We think that we're living in the land of the living on our way to the land of the dying, when in fact we are in the land of the dying on our way to the land of the living." We inhabit a dying, disintegrating planet, but we are on our way to a permanent and eternal world.

The Water of Life

So John writes in verse 1 of chapter 22 that "a pure river of water of life" flows through heaven. Now this river was first mentioned in Revelation 21:6 as "the fountain of the water of life," which God will give freely to anyone who is thirsty.

This is a glorious, crystal-clear, life-giving stream gushing from the throne of God. The psalmist pictured it prophetically as "a river whose streams shall make glad the city of God" (Ps. 46:4).

This resplendent river reflects the awesome presence and glory of the God who sits upon the throne of heaven. Here is an inexhaustible supply flowing from the presence of God. His love and grace will satisfy our thirst forever.

Contrast this with the burning thirst of hell, which Jesus told us about in Luke 16:24. The rich man begged for just a drop of water to cool his tongue. But in heaven the redeemed will drink forever from the wells of salvation, and they will never thirst again (see John 4:13–14).

The Tree of Life

Then in verse 2 of Revelation 22, John sees the "tree of life" growing in the midst of heaven. Now since this tree is said to grow on both sides of the river, most Bible commentators believe this refers to a great forest full of trees of life, bearing fruit every month.

When this heavenly fruit is eaten, it has a healing effect on "the nations," the inhabitants of heaven. Now since there is no sickness in heaven, this word *healing* is better understood as "healthful" or "health-giving." It is therapeutic.

That is what the word means, in fact, for the English word *therapeutic* is derived from it. In other words, this is "heavenly health food"! This has to do with renewed vitality and renewed strength. In some way we do not fully understand, the tree of life will contribute to our well-being in heaven.

In the Garden of Eden, Adam and Eve ate of the forbidden fruit in rebellion against God, and mankind was plunged into the darkness of the long night of sin. Our first parents were banished from Eden, cut off from the tree of life (Gen. 3:24).

Here in the presence of God, by the river of life, we will eat freely every day from this tree. We will enjoy fullness of life.

You say, "Are we going to eat in heaven?" Absolutely, amen, selah! I'm looking forward to the marriage supper of the Lamb. They're going to serve chicken-fried steak with mashed potatoes and gravy—and your cholesterol count won't go up a bit. It's going to be wonderful in this new location.

I heard about a Philadelphia lawyer who ordered two bouquets of flowers. He wanted one sent to a fellow attorney who was moving to a new location, and the other sent to a friend who had lost a family member.

Somehow the two orders got mixed up. The attorney received flowers at his new office with a note that said, "My deepest sympathy." The funeral home received flowers with a note that said, "Congratulations on your new location."

Well, Christian, congratulations on your new location! Your home is already prepared, just awaiting occupancy. Revelation 22:3 tells us that in this new location, "there shall be no more curse." The curse of sin is removed.

No More Curse

The whole creation is groaning under the burden of sin, eagerly waiting for the curse to be lifted (Rom. 8:19–22). This old earth bears the ugly scars and the dirty stains of sin.

There is pollution, flood, fire, thorns, thistles, disasters, disease, death—all a part of the curse.

In the new heaven and the new earth, all of that will be gone. The effects of sin will be forever reversed: no more violence, no more upheaval, no more contending with Satan. There will be no funeral processions up the streets of glory, no graves on the hillside of heaven.

The reason there is no more curse in heaven is that "the throne of God and of the Lamb shall be in it" (Rev. 22:3). Heaven will be governed by the triune God: God the Father, God the Son—the Lamb who was sacrificed for our sin—and God the Holy Spirit.

When you look into the face of God in the pure light of eternity, you will see the face of Jesus Christ. At His name "every knee should bow . . . [and] every tongue should confess that [He] is Lord, to the glory of God the Father" (Phil. 2:10–11). Jesus Christ the Lord will rule unrivaled.

In our times it looks as though God is getting the short end of a long stick. But in that day, Jesus Christ shall reign forever and ever.

Ceaseless Service to God

In case you are wondering what we are going to do throughout eternity in heaven, Revelation 22:3 says, "And His servants shall serve Him." The word here is *bondslaves*, and the verb is in the future tense. That means God's servants will "keep on and on" serving Him forever.

Earlier we talked about the fact that God has put within each one of us the drive to achieve, to do something productive and meaningful with our lives. It's part of being made in His image. We've all experienced the satisfaction of a job not only well done, but done for the right reasons.

What should motivate us in this life is the desire to do great things for God, to hear His "well done" when we stand before Him. But here on earth we serve so imperfectly. We fail; we get tired; we get frustrated; our motives are so often mixed.

In heaven, however, there will be none of that. Imagine serving someone you love perfectly, doing something that you enjoy preeminently, and doing it in a body that is forever energized.

We will serve the Lord continuously in heaven, with a pure heart and pure motivation, accomplishing great things for God. And we will never grow tired. Remember, there is no more night in heaven, so no need to sleep. We'll just keep serving God, and the more we serve Him the more we'll love it.

Don't think that when you get to heaven, they're going to issue you a harp, a halo, a woolly suit of long underwear, and then assign you a cloud so you can sit and strum and waste all eternity away!

You will serve the Lord endlessly and tirelessly. There will be no midlife crises, no burnout, no leveraged buyouts, and no downsizing forever.

You will be like the disciples when Jesus multiplied the loaves and the fish and they just kept handing it out. They didn't understand it, they didn't know how Jesus did it, but God supernaturally enabled them to keep serving.

Face-to-Face with Jesus

Look at verse 4 of Revelation 22. "They shall see His face, and His name shall be on their foreheads." In the Bible, name represents a person's character. In heaven, Jesus' name—His character, His righteousness—will be upon us. We will reflect His glory as we see Him face-to-face.

The ultimate bliss, the ultimate blessedness, the ultimate beauty of heaven will be to see Jesus face-to-face. Peter said that even though we have not yet seen Him, we love Him and rejoice with inexpressible joy (1 Peter 1:8). Since that's true down here, what will our joy be like when we see our Lord?

The same apostle John tells us elsewhere that when we see Jesus, "we shall be like Him, for we shall see Him as He is" (1 John 3:2). The psalmist said, "I shall be satisfied when I awake in Your likeness" (Ps. 17:15).

When we stand before Jesus in heaven, we will not see Him as the Galilean, the carpenter from Nazareth. We will see Him as John saw Him in Revelation 1:12–16, the blazing, glorified Lord ruling over His church and all of creation. His bright and blessed light will fill our lives with light forever.

This is why heaven needs "no lamp nor light of the sun" (Rev. 22:5). God just snuffs out the sun and the entire solar system. They're not necessary anymore, for Jesus Himself is the light of heaven. Then John says at the end of verse 5, "[We] shall reign forever and ever."

The glory of heaven is being face-to-face with Jesus Christ, worshiping and adoring and serving Him through the endless ages of eternity. Heaven wouldn't be heaven without Jesus. We will see Him as He is, we will be rewarded by Him, and we will reign with Him and serve Him world without end in His eternal kingdom.

That is heaven. No more night, no more sin, no more suffering, no more death.

Bringing Heaven to Earth

You may be saying, "This all sounds wonderful. Count me in on heaven. But what about today? I'm battling the darkness right now. The nights are getting longer and longer. I feel like John living on that lonely island. Can I get a little bit of heaven down here?"

Yes, you can! My friend, if you are a believer in the Lord Jesus Christ, the full interest and attention of heaven are focused on you right now. Let me illustrate what I'm talking about from the Old Testament, and then demonstrate it from the New Testament.

Do you remember the story of the prophet Elisha in 2 Kings 6? Israel was being attacked by the Syrians, but Elisha was used by God to warn the king of Israel. This infuriated the king of Syria, so he sent his army to surround the city of Dothan, where Elisha was (2 Kings 6:1–14).

The next morning, Elisha's servant got up and found the city surrounded by the army of Syria. This man started shaking in his sandals and said to Elisha, "Alas, my master! What shall we do?" (2 Kings 6:15).

Elisha replied, "Don't worry. We've got them outnumbered." Then he prayed, "'LORD, I pray, open his eyes that he may see.' Then the LORD opened the eyes of the young man, and he saw . . . the mountain was full of horses and chariots of fire all around Elisha" (2 Kings 6:17).

The angels of heaven had been charged with the assignment of protecting Elisha and his servant. Heaven was all around them. It was just invisible, until God allowed them to see into another dimension.

Look at Hebrews 12:1, which speaks of a great "cloud of witnesses" that surrounds us as we run the race of the

Christian life. What the writer of Hebrews saw by faith was the saints, including our friends and loved ones, who have completed their race and are cheering us on from heaven's grandstand.

So you have the attention of the eternal God, His holy angels, and myriads of saints upon you as you walk through the darkness. You have all the forces of heaven at your disposal to see you through the darkest night. All that's required to see heaven around you is the eye of faith.

Keep running the race, and soon the last shadow of night will be lifted forever!

A Closing Word

We have talked throughout this book about meeting God in the dark experiences of life. We have seen how God's saints turned to Him in the darkness and found His comfort and strength.

It's possible that when it comes to knowing God in a personal way, you would have to say, "Jack, I really don't know where I stand with Christ. When it comes to knowing Him personally, I'm in the dark."

Well, my friend, that's the last place I would want to leave you! So let me share with you how you can become a Christian and know for certain that you belong to Christ:

1. Salvation is a gift.

Romans 6:23 says, "For the wages of sin is death, but the gift of God is eternal life in Christ Jesus our Lord."

You cannot earn, learn, or deserve salvation. It is not a goal to achieve, but a gift to receive. Salvation is rooted in the mercy of God, not the merit of man.

Ephesians 2:8–9 says, "For by grace you have been saved through faith, and that not of yourselves; it is the gift of God, not of works, lest anyone should boast."

The word *grace* means gift. Salvation is freely provided by a God who loves you just the way you are. But there is a problem . . . .

2. Man is a sinner.

According to Romans 3:23, "All have sinned and fall short of the glory of God."

Every person has broken God's commandments. Though you may be a "good" person in the eyes of others, in your heart you know there is something wrong. We fall short of God's high standard, which is perfection (see Matt. 5:48).

No one is perfect. We have all sinned and therefore cannot save ourselves simply by living a good life. The very best you can do is not enough, because . . .

3. God is love, but He is also holy and must punish sin.

God loves you very much. But He cannot overlook your sin because He is holy. That means He is totally separate from sin.

Our sin separates us from God's love. Sin is God's enemy, and He hates it! If He were simply to dismiss our sin or let sinners into heaven, that would be a violation of His nature.

So we have a dilemma. How can God love us and, at the same time, judge our sin? The answer is the greatest news ever shared.

4. God solved the dilemma in the death and resurrection of Jesus Christ.

Jesus Christ made it possible for us to go to heaven by dying on the cross. He paid the price for our sins and purchased a place in heaven for us. He took our place of judgment.

"For [God] made [Christ] who knew no sin to be sin for us, that we might become the righteousness of God in Him" (2 Cor. 5:21). What does all of this mean?

5. Man can receive God's forgiveness of sin and the gift of eternal life by faith.

The Bible declares, "Believe on the Lord Jesus Christ, and you will be saved" (Acts 16:31). Only by faith can you know God's love and forgiveness.

You can receive Jesus Christ as your Savior right now by faith through prayer, which is an expression of faith. God is not so much concerned with your words as He is with the attitude of your heart. If you want to know Christ, go to Him right now and admit to Him that you are a sinner, and ask Christ to come into your life, forgive your sin, and take control. He will!

If you will mean business with God, you can have the assurance that He will answer your prayer and save you. "Most assuredly, I say to you, he who believes in Me has everlasting life" (John 6:47).

If you have never settled the issue of your eternal destiny, take that step of faith today. Step out of the darkness into the light of eternal life!